# Time to Test

# Bible Prophecy

## 16 Prophecies Now Rising

Craig Crawford
Copyright 2019

# Time to Test

*"When I heard,
my belly trembled;
my lips quivered at the voice:
rottenness entered into my bones,
and I trembled in myself,
that I might rest (escape)
in the Day of Trouble."
(Habakkuk 3:16)*

Unless otherwise identified, all Scripture quotations in this publication are taken from the New King James Version (NKJV) Bible. Copyright © 1982 and 1994, Thomas Nelson Publishers, Inc. All rights reserved.

Verses marked TLB are taken from The Living Bible, copyright 1971. Used by permission of Tyndale House Publishers, Inc., Wheaton, Illinois 60189. All rights reserved.

Italics were added by the author for emphasis.

Author: Craig Crawford

Time to Test Bible Prophecy: 16 Prophecies Now Rising

Copyright 2019

All rights reserved.

ISBN: 9781093171921

Portions of this book were excerpted and expanded from an earlier book "The Prophecies ... A Journey to the End of Time" by the same author.

# CONTENTS

| | | |
|---|---|---|
| 1. | TIME TO TEST | 9 |
| 2. | ISRAEL, JERUSALEM & GAZA | 13 |
| 3. | VIOLENCE AND IMMORALITY | 43 |
| 4. | LAWLESSNESS | 53 |
| 5. | LYING & DECEIVING | 65 |
| 6. | CHURCHES "FALLING AWAY" | 71 |
| 7. | FALSE PROPHETS | 91 |
| 8. | WARS AND RUMORS OF WAR | 97 |
| 9. | EARTHQUAKES, FAMINES, DISEASE | 103 |
| 10. | KNOWLEDGE & TRAVEL INCREASE | 111 |
| 11. | GLOBAL WEATHER EXTREMES | 117 |
| 12. | RUSSIA-IRAN & TURKEY | 123 |
| 13. | SYRIA & IRAQ | 149 |
| 14. | ROMAN EMPIRE REUNITING | 179 |
| 15. | GLOBAL GOVERNMENT & RELIGION | 185 |
| 16. | CHINA RISING | 205 |
| 17. | COMING PEACE PLAN FOR ISRAEL | 211 |
| 18. | GOD'S PROMISE | 215 |
| 19. | HOW TO TEST BIBLE PROPHECY | 225 |

## A Warning to the Watchmen

*All who believe in God's Word are considered "Watchmen"*

"And what I (Jesus) say (command) to you,
I say to *all:* "*WATCH!*"
(Mark 13:37) (We are to know the prophetic signs)

"When I (God) bring the sword upon a land,
And the people of the land take a man from their territory
And make him their watchman,
When he sees the sword coming upon the land,
If he blows the trumpet and warns the people,
Then whoever hears the sound of the trumpet
And does not take warning,
If the sword comes and takes him away,
His blood shall be on his own head.
He heard the sound of the trumpet,
But did not take warning;
His blood shall be upon himself.
But he who takes warning will save his life (in Heaven).
But if the watchman sees the sword coming
And does not blow the trumpet,
And the people are not warned,
And the sword comes and takes any person
from among them,
He is taken away (after death) in his iniquity (sin);
But his blood I will require at the watchman's hand."
(Ezekiel 33:2-9)

"When I say to the wicked, 'You shall surely die,'
And you give him no warning,
nor speak to warn the wicked
From his wicked way, *to save his life,*
That same wicked man shall die in his iniquity (sin);
But his blood I will require at your hand."
(Ezekiel 3:18)

*"For I am God, and there is no other.
I am God, and there is none like me,
Declaring the end from the beginning,
and from ancient times
things that are not yet done."*

*(Isaiah 46:9-10)*

*"Search from the book of the LORD,*
*And read:*
*Not one of these (prophecies) shall fail;*
*Not one shall lack her mate.*
*For My mouth has commanded it,*
*and His Spirit has gathered them."*
*(Isaiah 34:16)*

## TIME TO TEST BIBLE PROPHECY

*"The Bible is unlike any other book ever written."*

The Bible takes us from the very *Beginning* . . .

"In the beginning
God created the heavens and the Earth."
(Genesis 1:1)

To the very *End* . . .

"Now I saw a new heaven and a new Earth,
for the first heaven and the first earth
had passed away."
(Revelation 21:1)

Almost 30% of the Bible is prophetic (telling of future events), and has so far been 100% accurate.

The Bible says only God knows the end from the beginning. God uses prophecy to *prove* He is who He says He is, and to authenticate His message. There *is* no other book like it.

Few churches or synagogues today ever teach it or even want to discuss it. Many will say it's *already* past or just symbolic.

Prophecies are God's way of warning Mankind of the grave danger which now lies ahead. The Bible warns a single generation will see the fulfillment of many extraordinary prophecies, *beginning* with Israel being gathered back into her Land as a nation with Jerusalem as her capital once again ... and *ending* with the Rapture, Antichrist, the Apocalypse, Armageddon, and Messiah's Return.

*We believe that Generation is alive today!*

Bible Prophecy allows (and invites) everyone in the world, both the skeptical and the sympathetic, and the Christian and Non-Christian alike, to test God's Word.

Since Israel became a nation once again in 1948 (after 2,500 years) there has been a rising interest (and curiosity) in Bible Prophecy. Yet, today there are very few people who actually take these ancient prophecies seriously.

Can an ancient Book written 2,000-3,000 years ago now be accurately predicting today's news headlines and world events?

*Isaac Newton thought so.*

Sir Isaac Newton is one of the greatest scientists and mathematicians of all time. Besides his work on universal gravitation, his development of the Three Laws of Motion (which form the basic principles of modern Physics), and his discovery of Calculus (a powerful tool for solving Mathematical problems), Isaac Newton also intently studied Bible prophecy, and after great study and consideration he came to the following conclusion ...

> *"About the time of the end,*
> *a body of men will be raised up*
> *who will turn their attention to*
> *the prophecies of the Bible*
> *and insist on their literal interpretation*
> *in the midst of much clamor*
> *and opposition."*
>
> - Sir Isaac Newton -
> (1643-1727 A.D.)

Most people would probably agree God would not (or will not) fulfill His prophecies in secret, but so the whole world could see, and because we *are* now seeing such a growing body of men (and women) turning their attention to the prophecies of the Bible, it seems as though it might be a good (and reasonable) time *to test* these things by using whatever methods science, mathematics (and even good ol' common sense) can provide to objectively determine if these things are true, and if so, what do the prophecies of the Bible also say about *tomorrow's* headlines? For the Bible warns ... *our future is already history!*

The 16 Bible Prophecies you are about to read now all appear to be rising in this Generation. The Bible warns we would "see these things" around the time of the coming Apocalypse.

> *"Search from the Book of the LORD, and read:*
> *Not one* of these (prophecies) shall fail;
> *Not one* shall lack her mate."
> (Isaiah 34:16)

> "When you *see* these things,
> Know that it is *near* - -
> At the door!!"
> (Mark 13:29)

At the end of this book we will show you *how* to test these things using proven Scientific and Mathematical methods!

The answer to "WHY?" it is important to test these prophecies now is answered in the book "The $7^{th}$ Day Prophecy" which details and explains the Bible prophecies concerning the coming Antichrist, the Apocalypse, Armageddon, the Rapture (our Escape), Christ's Return, the Millennial Kingdom, and "the *New* Heaven and the *New* Earth" which the Bible tells us are coming.

# Time to Test

# ISRAEL, JERUSALEM & GAZA

*"He will set up a banner
for the nations,
and will assemble
the outcasts of Israel,
and gather together
the dispersed of Judah
from the four corners
of the Earth."
(Isaiah 11:12)*

## ISRAEL & JERUSALEM
### The Road to Armageddon

**On May 14, 1948 God's prophetic clock started ticking, *loudly!***

These prophecies are important because we can now watch the news, read a world history book, or look at a current map of the world and see there is now a nation called Israel. For almost 2,500 years - starting with the Jewish captivity under Babylon, then Persia, then Greece, then Rome; and, almost 2,000 years since the birth and rejection of the Messiah, when God held the children of Israel accountable, and then, using the Roman army, scattered the people into the nations around the world - the Jews have been dispersed. A people without a nation.

However, God said He would one day re-gather the children of Israel into the Land which He has given them as a nation. Through His prophets God also warned He would then judge them for profaning His Holy Name while scattered around the world. This prophetic re-gathering, which this generation is now seeing take place, is to serve as a sign and a warning to the world that the Apocalypse, the "Day of the Lord," draws near ...

> "He will set up a banner
>   for the nations,
>   and will assemble
>   the outcasts of Israel,
>   and gather together
>   the dispersed of Judah
>   from the four corners
>   of the Earth."
> (Isaiah 11:12)

"Thus says the Lord GOD:
  'Surely I will take
  the children of Israel
  from among the nations,
  wherever they have gone,
  and will gather them from every side
  and bring them into
  their own land;'"
(Ezekiel 37:21)

"And you, son of man,
  prophesy to the mountains of Israel,
  and say, 'O mountains of Israel,
  hear the word of the LORD...'
  But you, O mountains of Israel,
  you shall shoot forth your branches
  (Israel regathering into Her land)
  and yield your fruit
   to My people Israel,
  for they are about to come ..."
*"For I will take you (Israel)
from among the nations,
gather you out of all countries,
and bring you into your own land."*
(Ezekiel 36:1, 8, 24)

*"Who has heard such a thing?
Who has seen such things?
Shall the Earth be made
to give birth in one day?
Or shall a nation be born at once?
For as soon as Zion was in labor,
she gave birth to her children."*
(Isaiah 66:8)

*This prophecy WAS fulfilled in one day - May 14, 1948!*

**Now, search through history for nation Israel ...**

Year 500? ... "Nope."
Year 900? ... "Nope."
Year 1200? ... "Nope."
Year 1700? ... "Nope."
Year 1900? ... "Nope."
Year 1948? ... *"Yes!!!"* There it is ... on May 14, 1948!

How has the world reacted to such a profound fulfillment of Bible prophecy? A miracle that can be documented by simply looking at a map and a Bible. *It has ignored it!* Just as God says most of the world will ignore the warnings of the coming Apocalypse.

Remember, God uses prophecy to *prove* He is God, and to authenticate all the warnings and promises in the Bible.

*Jerusalem: "A Cup of Trembling"*

*God warns the battle over Israel and Jerusalem will continue to grow worse and worse ...*

"Behold, I (God) will make Jerusalem
a cup of trembling (anger, fear)
unto ALL the people (nations) round about . . ."
(Zechariah 12:2)

"And in that Day (the Apocalypse)
I (God) will make Jerusalem
a burdensome stone for ALL people"
(Zechariah12:3)

*Don't miss this!!* Through these prophetic verses, God is telling us *HE* is the One stirring things up in Israel and Jerusalem!!!

# Time to Test

# ALL NATIONS WILL UNITE AGAINST ISRAEL

*"For Behold,*

*In those days and at that time,*

*When I bring back the captives*

*of Judah and Jerusalem,*

*I will also gather ALL nations,*

*And bring them down*

*to the Valley of Jehoshaphat;*

*And I will enter into judgment with them there*

*On account of My people, My heritage Israel,*

*Whom they have scattered among the nations;*

*They have also divided up My land."*

*(Joel 3:1-3)*

# ALL NATIONS AGAINST ISRAEL

"For I (GOD)
*will gather ALL the nations
to battle against JERUSALEM"*
(Zechariah 14:2)

***The Bible warns around the time of the Apocalypse all of the nations of the world will unite against Israel!!***

The Bible warns *"At the time of the end"* (around the time of the coming Apocalypse and Armageddon, which is also called the "Time of Jacob's (Israel's) Trouble" (Jeremiah 30:7) *ALL* nations (including the United States) will unite (United Nations?) and turn against Israel (Zechariah 14:1-2 ... Joel 3:1-2 ... Revelation 16:13-16).

But, it is heart-wrenching to see it now actually happening. It is like watching the water receding from the beach just before a great and terrible tidal wave strikes.

**Remember ... Armageddon is in Israel.**

"For I (GOD)
*will gather ALL the nations
to battle against JERUSALEM"*
(Zechariah 14:2)

"And I (God)
will be to her (Jerusalem)
a wall of fire all around...
He who touches you (Jerusalem)
touches the apple (pupil) of His eye ...
(Woe to those who poke God in the eye)

Be silent, all flesh, before the Lord,
for He has roused Himself
from His holy dwelling"
(Zechariah 2:5,8,13)

## *Yet, God Promises ...*

*"I will BLESS those who bless you (Israel)
and will CURSE those who curse you."*
(Genesis 27:29 & Genesis 12:3 & Numbers 24:9)

# GAZA!!!

*"For GAZA shall be forsaken,*
*And Ashkelon desolate;*
*They shall drive out Ashdod at noonday,*
*And Ekron shall be uprooted."*
*(Zephaniah 2:1-2)*

# GAZA!!!

*"The Great Day of the LORD is near,
near and hastening fast;*
The sound of the Day of the LORD is bitter;
the mighty man cries aloud there.
A day of *wrath* is that Day,
A day of *distress* and *anguish*,
A day of *ruin* and *devastation*,
A day of *darkness* and *gloom*,
A day of *clouds* and *thick darkness*,
A day of *trumpet blast* and *battle cry*
against the fortified cities
and against the lofty battlements.
*I (GOD) will bring distress on Mankind,
so that they shall walk like the blind,
because they have sinned against the LORD;*
their blood shall be poured out like dust,
and their flesh like dung.
Neither their silver nor their gold
shall be able to deliver them
*on the Day of the Wrath of the LORD.
In the fire of His jealousy,
ALL the Earth shall be consumed;
For a full and sudden end
He will make of ALL the inhabitants of the Earth."*
(Zephaniah 1:14-18)

## PROPHECIES of GAZA

During August-September 2005 the world watched as all the Jews living in Gaza, including men, women, boys, and girls were forcibly removed from their homes and their land ...

Even those buried in cemeteries were dug up from their graves and removed from Gaza.

This 'uprooting' of the Jews from Gaza which the whole world watched on the news may be a much more significant prophetic event than most realize.

Through the prophet Zephaniah, God warned Gaza would one day be 'forsaken' (yes, that same Gaza you have recently been watching on the world news). Gaza is in the land which was given to the tribe of Judah (Joshua 15:1-12), and one of Messiah's titles *is* "The Lion of the Tribe of Judah" (Revelation 5:5).

*Through the following prophecies in the book of Zephaniah, God wants the children of Israel and ALL Mankind to learn and know at least THREE (3) things:*

**FIRST:**

*GOD has issued a terrible warning and a plea to both Israel and to ALL Mankind ...*

"Gather yourselves together,
Yes, gather together O undesirable nation
*Before* the decree is issued,
*Before* the Day passes like chaff,
*Before the Lord's fierce anger
comes upon you,
Before the Day of the Lord's anger
comes upon you!*
*Seek* the Lord, all you meek of the Earth
(this warning includes *all* Mankind)
who have upheld His justice
*Seek* righteousness,
*Seek* humility.
*It may be that you will be hidden
In the Day of the Lord's Anger (Wrath).*"
*(Study the prophecies of the coming 'Rapture')*
(Zephaniah 2:1-7)

## SECOND:

GOD wants all on Earth to know that *GAZA* will help trigger His fierce and terrible anger ("The Day of God's fierce anger and wrath").

*"Gaza will be Forsaken!"*

*"For GAZA shall be forsaken,*
And Ashkelon desolate;
They shall drive out Ashdod at noonday,
And Ekron shall be *uprooted.*
Woe to the inhabitants of the seacoast,
The nation of the Cherethites!
*The Word of the Lord* (A title of Jesus Christ - Messiah)
*is against you, O Canaan,*
*land of the Philistines (Palestinians):*
*"I (God) will destroy you*
*So there shall be no inhabitant."*
('Palestinians' and allies should take note)
(Zephaniah 2:1-7)

## THIRD:

*God also wants the children of Israel to know there is HOPE.*

He promises hope for all those who will endure in faith and trust in Jesus Christ (Yeshua Ha'Mashiach in Hebrew).

For one-day in the future, *after* the coming Apocalypse, which is also called "The Time of Jacob's (Israel's) Trouble," a remnant of the tribe of Judah will once again peacefully inhabit and prosper in that precious land God promised and gave to them.

Then, and only then, will there be "Peace on Earth." For at that time, God will restore all the Earth in peace and beauty ... *as promised.*

"The seacoast shall be pastures,
With shelters for shepherds
and folds for flocks.
*The coast shall be for the remnant
of the house of Judah;*
They (the remnant of the house of Judah)
shall feed there flocks there
(in the coastlands of Gaza);
In the houses of Ashkelon
they shall lie down at evening.
*The Lord their God
will intervene for them,
And return their captives."*
(Zephaniah 2:1-7)


***Some interesting things to note as we watch the news ...***

- *"Hamas"* took control over Gaza soon after Gaza was "forsaken" by Israel. Hamas is directed, trained, and equipped by Iran (study the prophecies of Russia and Iran).

- *"As the days of Noah"...*

Jesus warned the generation of the coming Apocalypse would be filled with "violence."

"But as the days of Noah were,
so *also* will the coming of the Son of Man be"
(Matthew 24:37)

To help us understand this prophecy, God *describes* the generation of Noah as morally "corrupt" and "filled with *violence.*"

**The actual Hebrew word translated "violence" in this passage is *"hamas!"***

"The Earth was corrupt before God,
(morally "corrupt"... like smelly, rotting meat)
*and the Earth was filled
with violence.*
(The Hebrew word for this violence was "hamas!")
So God looked upon the Earth,
and indeed it was (morally) corrupt;
for all flesh had corrupted
their way on the Earth.
And God said to Noah,
*"The end of all flesh
has come before Me,
for the Earth is filled
with violence* ('hamas')
through them;
and behold,
*I will destroy them
with the Earth.'"*
(Genesis 6:11-13)

In the Bible, God says He has given these prophecies and warnings so people will return to Him *before* the great and terrible Day of the Lord (the coming Apocalypse) in order to escape all these things which will come to pass.

With today's news and headlines, it may be a good time to start taking the Bible seriously.

*For Jesus Christ warns ...*

*"When you SEE
these things,
know that it is NEAR - -
At the DOOR!!"
(Mark 13:29)*

# MATHEMATICAL PROPHECY:

# ISRAEL

*"Who has heard such a thing?*
*Who has seen such things?*
*Shall the Earth be made*
*to give birth in one day?*
*Or shall a Nation be born at once?*
*For as soon as Zion was in labor,*
*she gave birth to her children."*
*(Isaiah 66:8)*

# THE PROPHETIC RETURN OF ISRAEL *and* JERUSALEM

*"Who has heard such a thing?
Who has seen such things?
Shall the Earth be made
to give birth in one day?
Or shall a Nation be born at once?
For as soon as Zion was in labor,
she gave birth to her children."
(Isaiah 66:8)*

**ISRAEL** *back* **as a Nation ... May 14, 1948!!!**

You are about to read one of the most fascinating and remarkable prophecies in the Bible. What makes it even more remarkable is what it implies. For when we realize how precisely this prophecy has been fulfilled after 2,500 years, we must realize all the Bible prophecies concerning Israel and the world including the coming 'Apocalypse,' the Battle of Armageddon, Messiah's Return, and the many promises and warnings concerning both Heaven and Hell will be fulfilled just as accurately and literally as the amazing prophecy presented here ...

## The Prophecy ... Ezekiel 4:4-6

"Then God said to Ezekiel,
'Now lie on your left side for 390 days
to show Israel will be punished for 390 years
by captivity and doom.
Each day you lie there represents
a year of punishment ahead for Israel.
Afterwards, turn over and lay on your right side
for 40 days, to signify the years of Judah's punishment.
Each day will represent one year . . .'"
(Ezekiel 4:4-6)


## This is a Mathematical Bible Prophecy

Although a little obscure (and sophisticated) this is one of the most fascinating prophecies found in the Bible.

Here, we find God telling Ezekiel that each day he (Ezekiel) lies on his side will represent one year of punishment for the nation Israel (Israel + Judah) because of their iniquities (sins) against God . . .

So, we have:

```
   390  days    Judgment against the 10 northern tribes 'Israel'
+   40  days    Judgment against the 2 southern tribes 'Judah'
=  430  years   Judgment against the nation of Israel
```

## The Fulfillment of the Prophetic Judgment Begins

In 606 B.C. Israel (Judah) was taken into captivity by Babylon for exactly 70 years ...

    **430**  years of judgment determined against nation Israel
-  **70**  years fulfilled during the Babylonian captivity
= **360**  years remaining in judgment against nation Israel

## The Mystery of 360 Years

There should have been a total of 360 years left in judgment against Israel after their release from Babylonian captivity by the Persian general Cyrus, exactly 70 years after the Babylonian captivity began (just as the prophet Jeremiah had prophesied before the captivity) ... but where was the remaining 360 year judgment in Israel's history??!!

## The 7X Factor of God's Judgment

Bible scholars could not find any specific captivity or dispersion that fulfilled these 360 years left in the judgment until a close look in the book of Leviticus revealed a startling prophetic warning ...

"And after all this,
  if you do not obey Me,
  then I (God) will punish you *seven times* more
  for your sins."
(Leviticus 26:18)

"Then, if you walk contrary to Me,
  and are not willing to obey Me,
  I (God) will bring on you *seven times* more plagues,
  according to your sins."
(Leviticus 26:21)

"And after all this,
  if you do not obey Me,
  but walk contrary to Me,
  then I (God) also will walk contrary to you in fury;

and I, even I will chastise you *seven times* for your sins.: (Leviticus 26:27-28)

*"I (God) will scatter you among the nations*
*and draw a sword after you;*
*your Land shall be desolate*
*and your cities waste."*
(Leviticus 26:33)

The 7X factor of God's judgment against nation Israel. God warned Israel if they continued in their disobedience He would multiply their judgment by seven times! Remember, as noted throughout these prophetic studies, God says what He means and He means what He says!

**Prophecy Fulfilled**

Now, let's apply the 7X factor to the remaining 360 years of judgment against nation Israel in this remarkable mathematical prophecy . . .

```
    360   Remaining years of judgment
  x   7   The prophetic '7X' factor
= 2,520   Years of judgment remained against nation Israel
```

God gave the Jews the most sophisticated calendar on Earth. It is both a Lunar and a Solar calendar. The Jewish calendar uses a 360 day lunar (and prophetic) year and then adds a 'Leap Month' on specific years to accurately coincide with the Solar cycle we use on our 'Julian' calendar ...

The Bible uses 360 day years for prophecies and expects us to add the appropriate 'leap months' on schedule. So, the easiest way to unravel this prophecy is to first convert this prophecy into days ...

```
    2,520  years
   x  360  days
= 907,200  days
```
of judgment remained against nation Israel after the Babylonian captivity

Now, to convert the 907,200 days found in this prophecy into our 365.25 day solar (Julian) years (the .25 adjusts for leap years) . . .

*2,483.78 years of God's judgment remained ...*

907,200 days ÷ 365.25 days = 2,483.78 years

**With this information, let's look at this remarkable prophecy again ...**

```
    606   B.C      Israel taken into Babylonian captivity
 -   70   Years    For 70 years
 =  536   B.C.     End of first 70 years of judgment
 + 2483   Years    Now add the 2,483 years remaining
 +    1   Year     Add 1 year for no "0" B.C. or A.D.
 = 1948   AD!!!    End of judgment against nation Israel
```

## *Israel Back in Her Land as a Nation ... in 1948!*

Judah (Israel) was taken into captivity by the Babylonians in 606 B.C. They were released from captivity 70 years later by the Persians in 536 A.D., exactly as the prophet Jeremiah had prophesied, but their land was still under the control of the Persians.

The Persians were later conquered by the Greeks, and the land of Israel remained under Greek control. The Greeks were then conquered by Rome and the land of Israel remained under Roman control.

After failed rebellions against Rome around 70 A.D. and another around 100 years later, the Romans removed the Jews from the land of Israel, dispersed them around the world and then renamed the land 'Palestine' after the enemies of Israel.

Then, after 2,500 years, and for the first time since the Babylonian captivity in 606 B.C., the world watched as Israel once again appeared on the world map as a sovereign nation, on May 14, 1948 ... exactly when the Bible said it would!

> "Thus says the Lord God:
> *'Surely I will take the children of Israel*
> *from among the nations,*
>   wherever they have gone,
>   and will gather them from every side
>   and bring them into their own land."
> (Ezekiel 37:21)

The prophecy says 'nations' (plural) ... this is *not* their return from Babylon.

# MATHEMATICAL PROPHECY: JERUSALEM

# Time to Test

# JERUSALEM BACK AS ISRAEL'S CAPITAL IN 1967

## JERUSALEM back as Israel's Capital ...

JERUSALEM!!!.

What makes this mathematical Bible prophecy concerning Jerusalem even *MORE* remarkable is if you take the *same* prophetic time-line we discovered with Israel being regathered as a nation once again for the first time in 2,500 years, which started on the year of Babylon's conquest of the nation Israel and ending with Israel once again raised as a nation in 1948, and now shift that *exact same prophetic time-line* to start on the year (and day) when Babylon *returned* and then destroyed the City of Jerusalem and the Temple 19 years later, we remarkably discover this prophetic time-line's "end-point" now falls on the *exact* year Israel once again regained sovereign control over *Jerusalem* in 1967 (after the "Six Day War.")

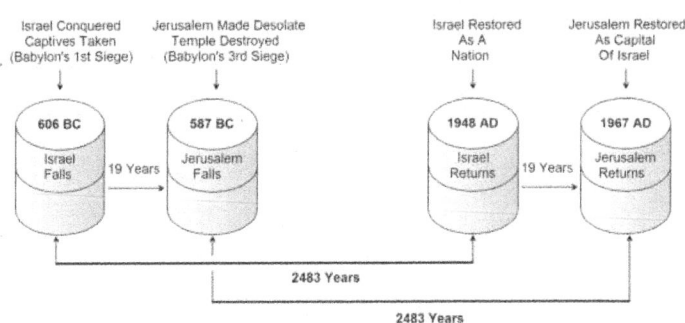

For a more precise study of this remarkable prophetic fulfillment of Ezekiel's prophecy in 1948 and 1967 read here ... Ezekiel's 430 day prophecy - Detailing the length of the "Desolations of Jerusalem" and the "Servitude of the Nation"- (Chuck Missler K-House Bible study)

internet

# VIOLENCE & IMMORALITY

*"But as the days of Noah were, so also will the coming of the Son of Man be ..."*
*(Matthew 24:37)*

# THE RISE OF VIOLENCE & IMMORALITY

*"WOE to those
who call evil good, and good evil;
Who put darkness for light,
and light for darkness."
(Isaiah 5:20)*

**The Rise of Violence and Immorality**

God has spent a lot of time and effort describing and warning of a single generation which would one day rise to see the terrible realities and consequences of ignoring and rejecting God's Word and His many warnings in prophecy. We are told these prophecies are His way of preparing Mankind for the grave danger which now lies ahead, while *also* offering us a way *"to ESCAPE all these things which will come to pass."* (The coming "Rapture" for all who are found waiting in faith. A detailed study can be found in the book "The 7th Day Prophecy" by the same author).

Much information is given in the Bible concerning the character, morals, and attitudes of the generation which will lead the world down into the terrors of the coming Apocalypse and Armageddon.

In the following prophecy, Jesus Christ warns the generation of the Apocalypse will be *just like* the generation living in the days of Noah, which God utterly destroyed with the Flood.

We will find there are *TWO* aspects to this prophecy which are important to learn and to understand ...

**FIRST:**

**The Generation of Armageddon will be morally corrupt and filled with violence**

*Jesus warns ...*
"But as the days of Noah were,
  so *also* will the coming
  of the Son of Man be ..."
(Matthew 24:37)


*To help us understand this part of the prophecy, God DESCRIBES the generation of Noah ...*

"*The Earth was (morally) CORRUPT before God,*
  (the Bible uses the word "corrupt" like smelly, rotting meat)
  *And the Earth was filled with VIOLENCE.*
  So God looked upon the Earth,
  and indeed it was corrupt;
  for all flesh had corrupted their way on the Earth.
  *And God said to Noah,*
  *'The end of all flesh has come before Me,*
  *for the Earth is filled with violence through them;*
  *and behold, I will destroy them*
  *with the Earth.'*"
(Genesis 6:11-13)


*So, our first prophetic clue is the Generation of Armageddon will be filled with violence and immorality.*

## SECOND:

## Most of the generation will *not* realize the Apocalypse is near, and will *not* be prepared

*"But as the days of Noah were,*
*so also will the coming of the Son of Man be.*
For as in the days before the flood,
they were eating and drinking,
marrying and giving in marriage,
UNTIL the day that Noah entered the Ark,
*and did NOT know until the Flood came*
*and took them all away,*
*so also will the coming of the Son of Man be.*
Then two men will be in the field:
*One will be taken and the other left.*
(The *escape* ... the coming "Rapture")
Two women will be grinding at the mill:
*One will be taken and the other left.*
(Lovingly *removed* ... *before* the Apocalypse)
*WATCH therefore!*
For you do not know what hour
your Lord is coming.
*But know this,*
that if the master of the house
had known what hour the thief would come,
he would have watched and not allowed
his house to be broken into.
*Therefore you also be ready,*
*for the Son of Man is coming at an hour*
*you do not expect."*
(Prophecies tell us *what* to look *and* then to *"Watch!"*)
(Matthew 24:37-44)

We are told that all those who are found waiting in faith will *"escape"* the Apocalypse.

**Some valuable insight ...**

Just before bringing disaster upon Israel with a catastrophic judgment, God gave his prophets (and us) some valuable insight into determining when a generation has crossed His line of moral corruption.

***God reveals to Jeremiah ...***

"They were *not* at all ashamed,
 *they did not even know how to BLUSH"*
 (Jeremiah 6:15 & Jeremiah 8:12)

***How many people do you know today over the age of 12 who still know how to blush?***

The character of a generation is not only revealed or reflected by the news reports of global violence and immorality which we read about daily, but, it is also revealed by what *entertains* a generation. Simply look at the movies, television shows, video games, and internet sites to see what now entertains this generation today.

God *also* warns there will come a time just before the catastrophic judgment when a generation will no longer receive Godly warnings from the pulpits, and most of the people will be blindly unaware of the grave danger which now lies ahead.

***God reveals an important prophecy to Amos ...***

"Behold, the days are coming," says the Lord GOD,
 That I will send a FAMINE on the land,
 *NOT* a famine of bread,
 *NOR* a thirst for water,
 *But of HEARING the words of the LORD."*
 (Amos 8:11)

It is somewhat analogous to a tidal wave. When we see the water rapidly receding from the shore we know it's the sign a massive tidal wave which will destroy and devastate everything in its path is rapidly approaching. In our scenario, the water represents the teaching (and hearing) of the Word of God, the shore represents our churches and synagogues, and the devastating Tidal Wave represents the coming Apocalypse ... the fierce and terrible *"Day of the Lord."*

**Jesus warns ...**

*"When you SEE these things,
know that it is NEAR - -
at the DOOR!!"*
(Mark 13:29)

Most people *can't* see because they don't know (and have never been taught) *what* to look for. Unfortunately, (and just as the Bible predicted), most of our churches and synagogues today either ignore, reject, or (for lack of knowledge) simply *avoid* God's prophetic word, even though Bible Prophecy represents somewhere around *25-30% of the whole Bible!*

*Jesus warned of the religious leaders in His day who ignored all of the prophetic signs of His first coming ...*

*"They are blind leaders of the blind.
And if the blind leads the blind,
both will fall into a ditch."*
(Matthew 15:14)

***How many churches (or synagogues) can you find today who ever teach any of the many prophetic signs we are told to diligently "watch" for concerning His return?***

Later, God gave Peter (and us) some valuable insight into how to identify the generation which will one day face the *final* catastrophic judgment upon the Earth.

**God reveals to Peter ...**

"*Knowing this first:*
*That SCOFFERS will come in the last days,*
(Many of these will go to church every Sunday)
walking according to their own lusts, and saying, '
*Where is the promise of His coming?*
For since the fathers fell asleep, all things continue on as they were from the beginning of creation.'"
(2 Peter 3:3-4)

God warns *many* will scoff at prophecies of Christ's Return.

**So, our second prophetic clue is the Generation of Armageddon will be ignorant of the Bible Prophecies, and will not believe (or will even mock or ridicule) those who do take God's warnings seriously.**

**The Bible now lists even *more* character traits which will mark the Generation of Armageddon ...**

"But *know* this,
 *that in the last days*
 *perilous* times will come,
 *For men will be* (Men = Mankind ... both men *and* women)
 Lovers of *themselves,*
 Lovers of *money,*
 *Boasters,*
 *Proud,* ("*Nobody* is going to tell *me* what to do!!")
 *Blasphemers,* (mocking and joking about God and Jesus)
 *Disobedient to parents,* (will not respect *any* authority)
 *Unthankful,*

*Unholy,*
*Unloving,*
*Unforgiving,*
*Slanderers,*
*Without Self-Control,*
*Violent* (brutal),
*Despisers of good,*
*Traitors,* (We are now seeing this rising rapidly)
*Headstrong,*
*Arrogant* (haughty),
*Lovers of Pleasure* (feeding desires of the 'flesh and eyes')
rather than lovers of God,
(placing their pleasures and possessions above God)
having a FORM of godliness
(professing a belief ... even going to church or synagogue)
*but denying its power ... "*
(God's power to help, heal, save, or even destroy)
(2 Timothy 3:1-5)

Unfortunately, most of those born after 1967 will have a very difficult time realizing these character traits aren't normal, or that there ever *was* any difference in how people generally acted, spoke, and behaved. While those born in the 1950's or before *can* see and realize what a stark difference there is now in the generation alive today compared to those which came before. Yet, it was mainly those born between 1948 and 1960 who were powerfully seduced, led, and then swept into the darkness of this "new morality," which quickly *changed* the way churches (and synagogues) began to teach and follow God's Word.

# LAWLESSNESS

*"And what will be the sign of Your coming, and of the end of the Age?"*

*"Jesus answered and said ... "Because LAWLESSNESS will abound, the love of many will grow cold"*
*(Matthew 24:3-4)*

# LAWLESSNESS
# A SIGN OF THE APOCALYPSE

## The Generation of Armageddon will be marked by 'Lawlessness'

"Now as He (Jesus) sat on the Mount of Olives,
  the disciples came to Him privately, saying,
"Tell us, when will these things be?
  *And what will be the sign of Your coming,
  and of the end of the Age?"*
And Jesus answered and said to them: ...
"And because *LAWLESSNESS* will abound,
  the love of many  (for Jesus Christ and the Word of God)
  will grow cold.
  *But he who endures (in faith) to the end
  shall be saved*  (into the Kingdom of Heaven).
  And this Gospel ("good news") of the Kingdom
  will be preached in all the world
  as a witness to all the nations,
  *and THEN the end will come."*  (The coming Apocalypse)
(Matthew 24:3-4...12-14)

## Jesus warns *many* who call themselves Christians will practice Lawlessness

*"NOT everyone who says to Me, 'Lord, Lord,'
  shall enter into the Kingdom of Heaven.*
  (These people consider themselves Christians)
  *MANY* ('most' or 'majority' who call themselves Christian)
  will say to Me in that Day (of Judgment)
  *'Lord, Lord,* have we not taught (prophesied)
  in Your Name,
  cast out demons in Your Name,
  and done many wonders in Your Name?
  (They may have been very busy in church)

And then (at the Judgment)
I (Jesus) will declare to them
*'I never knew you,* (through love, faith, trust, and obedience)
*DEPART from Me* (out of Heaven)
*you who practice Lawlessness.'"*
(Matthew 7:21-23)

**ANOTHER *prophetic warning against 'Lawlessness'* ...**

*"The Son of Man* (Jesus ... see Daniel 7:13-14)
*will send out His angels,*
and they will gather out of His Kingdom
All things that offend,
*and those who practice Lawlessness,*
and will cast them into the furnace of fire.
*There will be wailing and gnashing of teeth."*
(Matthew 13:41-42)

**'Lawlessness' *IS* a major prophetic sign**

One objective here is to simply provide a mechanism to help people *test* to see if Bible Prophecies are now being fulfilled (or preparing to be fulfilled) in this generation. As we read above, the Bible warns "Lawlessness will abound."

Lawlessness refers to large segments of a generation *defying, ignoring, or rejecting* God's Law as found in the Bible. We will also see it even applies to those who just "approve of those" who do such things.

**So, another prophetic sign of the coming Apocalypse is the Generation alive at the time will abound with Lawlessness.**

Keeping this in mind, there are two rising social issues that are worth looking into and considering from a *Biblical* perspective. Could these current social issues qualify as prophetic "Lawlessness?"

**What *does* the Bible (God's Law) say about Homosexuality and Abortion?**

The objective here is not to force God's Will upon a person in order to agree or disagree with God's Law (for God has given us all a free will to make our own decisions in life), but, it is simply to help people determine what the Bible actually says about these things.

Each reader needs to objectively decide on their own whether these current social issues (which we have seen rise to prominence so quickly in this generation) would qualify as "Lawlessness" from both a Biblical *and* Prophetic perspective.

**HOMOSEXUALITY:**

***What DOES the Bible (God's Law) say about Homosexuality?***

"You shall not lie with a male as with a woman.
It is an abomination."
(Leviticus 18:22)

"If a man lies with a male as he lies with a woman,
both of them have committed an abomination.
They shall surely be put to death.
Their blood shall be upon them."
(Leviticus 20:13)

"A woman shall not wear anything that pertains to a man,
nor shall a man put on a woman's garment,
for all who do so are an abomination
to the LORD your God."
(Deuteronomy 22:5)

"Do you not know that the unrighteous
will *NOT* inherit the Kingdom of God"
*Do not be deceived.*
Neither fornicators, (any sex outside of marriage)
nor adulterers,
*nor homosexuals,*
*nor sodomites,*
nor thieves, ...
will inherit the Kingdom of God.
And such *were* some of you. (We are *all* sinners)
But you were *washed*
(by the innocent blood of Jesus shed for all our sins)
But you were *sanctified*
(sanctified means "set apart")
But you were *justified*
(justified means "just as if your sins had never happened")
*in the Name of the Lord Jesus*
*and by the Spirit of our God."*
(1 Corinthians 6:9-11)


**In the following passage we find the Bible goes on to warn that God's Law also applies to those who simply "Approve of" these things ...**

"For the wrath of God
is revealed from Heaven
against all ungodliness
and unrighteousness of men . . .
For even their women
exchanged the natural use
for what is against nature (lesbianism).
Likewise also the men,
leaving the natural use of the woman,
burning in their lust or one another,

men with men committing
what is shameful (homosexuality) ...
that those who practice these things
are worthy of death (Hell),
*And not only those who do the same*
*but also those who **approve of** those who practice them!"*
(Romans 1:18, 26, 27, 32)
(Other offenses were also included which are not listed.)

In the verse above, we are given a Godly warning to all those who simply *"approve of"* these things will be held just as accountable as those who actually do them. We will find in a later chapter this also applies to churches and church leaders.

***Bible Prophecy ALSO warns that Sodom and Gomorrah were given as "examples" and warnings for a future generation ...***

"As Sodom and Gomorrah,
and the cities around them
in a similar manner to these,
(a total of 5 cities were destroyed)
having given themselves over to sexual immorality
and gone after strange flesh, (homosexuality)
*are set forth as an EXAMPLE,*
suffering the vengeance of eternal fire."
(Jude 1:7)

"And turning the cities of
Sodom and Gomorrah into ashes,
condemned them (Sodom and Gomorrah) to destruction,
*making them an EXAMPLE*
to those who *afterward*
would live ungodly ..."
(2 Peter 2:6)

Taken from *both* the Old *and* New Testaments, all the verses above relating to homosexuality are given because they represent a portion of God's Law as found in the Bible from both a Jewish and a Christian point of view.

The verses we have just read also reveal God's Law is *not* ambiguous concerning homosexuality. If we do our homework, we will discover that Homosexuality is nothing new. At the time the Apostle Paul wrote the verses above homosexuality was rampant throughout the ancient Roman Empire. Roman Emperor Nero once married a man who was dressed as the bride, and on another occasion, Emperor Nero himself dressed as the bride as he married another man. However, the generation alive today is the first generation since the fall of the ancient Roman Empire to embrace, promote, and approve of homosexuality in such a decisive and overt manner.

Since the objective here is to provide the reader with a relevant and timely selection of Bible Prophecies in order to help test to see if we *are* getting close to the coming Apocalypse, it is up to each individual reader to determine for themselves whether or not these current social issues are prophetically significant.

## ABORTION:

### *What DOES the Bible say about Abortion?*

"Were your acts of harlotry
a small matter,
that you have slain
*MY* children,
(God sees these babies as His!)
and offered them up
to them (demons)
by causing them
to pass through the fire ..."
(Ezekiel 16:20-21)

"And you shall not
let any of your descendants
pass through the fire
to Molech."
(Leviticus 18:21)

*"By causing them (babies) to pass through the fire"*... Back then, unwanted babies were "offered" to a false god Molech (a demon-god of lust and pleasure) by placing the baby onto the glowing red-hot arms of a small bronze statue which was placed in the fire.

God says *a lot* about this killing of unwanted babies (sometimes described as "passing sons and daughters through the fire" and "shedding innocent blood") in the Bible. As we discover in the verses above, God sees it and it causes Him to cry out in agony and in anger.

It is also important to note that from an historical perspective, the controversy surrounding "Abortion" goes back *thousands* of years.

## *We find this issue mentioned in the book of Psalms ...*

*"They sacrificed their sons
and their daughters
to the demons; (Molech)
they poured out innocent blood,
the blood of their sons and daughters,*
whom they sacrificed
to the idols of Canaan,
and the land
was polluted with blood.
Thus they became unclean
by their acts,
and played the whore in their deeds.
*Then the anger of the LORD
was kindled against His people,*
and He abhorred His heritage;
He gave them (Israel)
into the hand of the nations, (Assyria and Babylon)
so that those who hated them
ruled over them."
(Psalms 106:37-40)


## Quotes from the ancient Christian Church fathers

*In the following passages (including the years which they were written) which have been excerpted from Dr. Ken Johnson's book "The Ancient Church Fathers" (pp. 132-135) we discover the controversy surrounding abortion goes back thousands of years ...*

Didache, AD 100
Chapter 2 - "You shall not murder a child by abortion, nor kill them when born."

Barnabas, AD 100
Epistle of Barnabas 19-12 - "You shall not murder a child by abortion, nor shall you kill it when it is born.

Tertullian, AD 200
Apology 9 - In our case, murder being once for all forbidden, we may not destroy even the fetus in the womb, while as yet the human being derives blood from other parts of the body for its sustenance. To hinder a birth is merely a speedier man-killing.

Nations 1.15 - Christians do not kill infants before or after birth.

Treatise of the Soul 1.25 - Heretics maintain that the soul is not conceived in the womb. They maintain that the soul is deposited much later, after conception. Christians teach abortion is murder.

Treatise of the Soul 1.26 - Among surgeons' tools there is a certain instrument that is formed with a nicely-adjusted flexible frame for first of all opening the uterus and then keeping it open. It also has a circular blade, by means of which the limbs within the womb are dissected with careful but unflinching care. Its last appendage is a blunted or covered hook, by which the entire fetus is extracted by a violent delivery. There is also a copper needle or spike, by which the actual death is brought about in their treacherous robbery of life. From its infanticide function, they give the name, "killer of the infant" – which infant, of course, had once been alive.

Hippolytus, AD 206
Against Heresies 9.7 - Women who were reputed believers began to resort to drugs for producing sterility. They also girded themselves around, so as to expel what was being conceived. For they did not wish to have a child by either a

slave or by any common fellow – out of concern for their family and their excessive wealth. See what a great impiety the Lawless One has advanced. He teaches adultery and murder at the same time.

For our purposes, these early Church writings appear to support the position that Abortion *would* be considered against God's Law, and therefore could qualify as a prophetic form of "Lawlessness," which *is* a key and important component found in these Bible Prophecies we are studying and presenting for review.

As mentioned earlier, these important Bible Prophecies studies are given in order to help determine whether or not the generation alive today is (or could be) the prophetic generation which will enter into the dark terrors of the Apocalypse and Armageddon.

It is up to each individual reader to objectively determine for themselves whether or not these issues, or any of the social and global issues presented in these studies, should or should not be considered *prophetically* significant.

# Lying, Deceiving & Being Deceived

*"But KNOW this,
that in the last days
perilous times will come ...
Evil men and impostors
will grow worse and worse,
DECEIVING (lying)
and being deceived."
(2 Timothy 3:1, 13)*

## LYING & DECEIVING

*What DOES the Bible say about Lying and Deceiving?*

*The Bible warns God hates lying ...*

"*These six things
the Lord hates,
Seven that are detestable to Him ...*
- A proud look (arrogance, selfishness, conceit)
- *A lying tongue*
- Hands that shed innocent blood
- A heart that devises sinful plans
- Eagerness and willingness to do wrong
- A false witness *speaking lies*
- One who sows discord among brethren
(Proverbs 6:16)

**"In the Last Days"**

The Bible warns *"in the last days"* (around the time of the coming Apocalypse) a generation of evil men and women would rise. We are told that lying, deceiving, and being deceived will *characterize* that generation (and its leaders) who will lead the world into the coming Apocalypse. To help clarify the terminologies, it should be noted that 'lying' and 'deceiving' are a little different. Deceiving is considered *worse* than lying because deceiving (deception) *mixes some truth* in with the lie, which makes it much more difficult to discern the lie.

## *The Bible is very adamant about knowing this prophecy ...*

"But *KNOW* this,
that in the last days
perilous times will come . . .
*Evil men* and impostors (Mankind ... men and women)
*will grow worse and worse,*
DECEIVING *(lying)*
*and being deceived."*
(2 Timothy 3:1, 13)

The Bible tells us God cannot lie and that He hates all lies.

God says truth is non-negotiable and is fundamental to His Law. In fact, the Bible tells us at least five times it is *"impossible"* for God to lie.

In the past, liars and perjurers were held accountable and dealt with harshly and severely. Today we see lying casually accepted in the news, in the movies, and on television. Lying is now being presented as funny and harmless. This generation is unique in its reaction to liars and perjurers. This nation even lifted up a recent President whose most notable characteristic was revealed by flagrantly staring into a TV camera and wagging his finger while blatantly lying to the whole nation. Even though later convicted for criminal perjury he is still a very popular leader.

Many in this generation today mock our nation's Rules of Law. Many now also mock God's Law. As noted, telling the truth is fundamental to God's Law. In the Bible we find when a nation and its leaders defiantly mock, ignore, and turn their backs on God's Law, the future of that nation and people is always very, very grim ...

## Serious Warnings ...

*"Knowing this:*
that the Law is not made for a righteous person,
but for the Lawless and insubordinate,
for the ungodly and for sinners,
for the unholy and profane,
for murderers of fathers and murderers of mothers,
for manslayers,
for sexually immoral (fornicators),
for homosexuals (sodomites),
for kidnappers,
*for LIARS,*
*for perjurers,*
and if there is any other thing
that is *contrary* to sound doctrine."
(1 Timothy 1:8-10)

"But the cowardly,
unbelieving,
abominable,
murders,
sexually immoral,
sorcerers ("pharmakeus"... includes both occult and drugs)
idolaters,
AND ALL LIARS
*shall have their part*
*in the lake which burns*
*with fire and brimstone,*
*which is the second death."* (Hell)
(Revelation 21:8)


Please remember, the Bible clearly says God is a forgiving God who will forgive any and all who have sinned against Him. The Bible tells us we are *all* sinners who can be lovingly and completely forgiven.

# Time to Test

# CHURCHES "FALLING AWAY"

*"Now the Holy Spirit expressly says that in latter times some (churches and church leaders) will depart from the faith"*
*(1 Timothy 4:1)*

# CHURCHES

# "FALLING AWAY"

*"Now the Holy Spirit expressly says
that in latter times some
(churches and church leaders)
will depart from the faith"*
*(1 Timothy 4:1)*

### What *IS* the "Apostasy"?

The term "depart" from the faith which we find in many of our Bible translations comes from the Greek word aphistemi (apostasy), which literally means "to stand away from God's Word," and denying that which is professed as truth in the Bible.

### The "Falling Away" of the Churches:

**The Bible warns in *"the latter times"* churches will *"depart from the faith"* and will *"no longer endure sound doctrine."***

*From Bible prophecies we find this "falling away" (Apostasy) would begin with 'some' churches which would then grow into 'many' churches as we approach the coming Apocalypse. After the Rapture it will become 'all' churches (the great Apostasy) ...*

*"Now the Holy Spirit expressly says*
   (This is *God* warning us)
   *that in LATTER times some*
   *(churches and church leaders)*
   *will DEPART from the faith,*
   giving heed to deceiving spirits

and doctrines of demons
(denying and opposing God's Law in the Bible)
speaking lies in hypocrisy,
having their own conscience
seared (numbed) with a hot iron,
forbidding to marry ..."
(1 Timothy 4:1-3)

"Beloved, (he is speaking to believing Christians)
while I was very diligent to write to you
concerning our common salvation,
I found it necessary ("compelled")
to write to you exhorting you
to contend earnestly for the faith
which was once for all delivered to the saints.
*For certain men (and women)*
*have crept in unnoticed, (church leaders)*
*who long ago were marked out*
*for this condemnation,*
ungodly men (and women),
who turn the grace of our God
into lewdness.
*But I want to remind you,*
though you once knew this,
that the Lord, having saved the people
out of the land of Egypt,
afterward destroyed those
who did *not* believe (God's Word)."
(God's Laws are the same for every generation.)
(Jude 1:3-6)

*"For the time will come*
when they
(churches, church leaders, and many Christians)
*will NOT endure sound doctrine.*
*Instead,* to suit their own desires,
*they will gather around them*

*a great number of teachers
to say what their itching ears
WANT to hear.*
(and not what the Bible says)
They will turn their ears
*away* from the truth (as found in God's Word)
and turn aside to myths."
(such as the 'DaVinci Code')
(2 Timothy 4:3-5)

**These crucial Bible prophecies and warnings were written for those attending churches in the "*latter*" times**

The problem is not many people today really *want* to hear what the Bible has to say.

Few will take the time to learn what the Bible actually teaches (or warns) about many of these serious social issues which are now confronting (and testing) this generation. A deeper knowledge and understanding of God's Word could quickly eliminate much of the anger (or confusion) concerning these things which are dividing many people, churches, and Christians today. Yet, more and more people are basing their knowledge and understanding of God's Word solely on whatever their church or church leaders are choosing to tell them. The Bible warns against developing a higher degree of love and loyalty toward a particular church or church leader than toward God and God's Word.

*The Apostle Paul praised the Berean churchgoers because they would eagerly listen to their church leader (and Paul), but would then go home to "search the Scriptures daily" to see if what they were being taught was true ...*

"The Bereans were more fair-minded
  than those in Thessalonica,
   in that they received the word (heard the sermon)

with great eagerness,
*but then SEARCHED the Scriptures daily
to find out whether these things (they were being taught)
were true."*
(Acts 17:11)

The danger in *not* holding our local churches accountable to the Scriptures is that people can quickly be led to *replace* the sincere love for (and obedience to) God's Word which God seeks and desires, with a socialized or "works-based" form of Christianity. Even though all Christians *should* be doing good works in loving, helping, forgiving, and sharing with others as proof of their faith (while also enjoying the friendships and social benefits which can be found when regularly attending a church), we have to remember that our good works (or social activities) can *never save us* into Heaven ... (but, we are promised *rewards* for them in Heaven).

Believing Christians know Jesus Christ *is* God who stepped forth from eternity ("From of old, from everlasting" - Micah 5:2) in order to suffer and die for *our* sins so we can be "washed clean" of all of our sins by His blood shed on the Cross and then clothed in *His* perfect righteousness, through faith. We are promised if we turn *away* from those sins ("repent") which He suffered and died for, and place all of our faith and trust in Jesus having paid the terrible price for *all* of our sins (past, present, and future) upon the Cross, and believe He rose from the dead on the third day (to offer *us* a new and eternal life), we will have the full assurance (and God's promise) of everlasting life in Heaven.

God's Word also teaches the Greatest Commandment is to love God above all other things. Now consider the fact that Jesus Christ is not only God manifest in human flesh, but in John 1:1 and Revelation 19:13 we *also* find Jesus Christ is the "*WORD* of God."

***So, when Jesus (God) says ...***

*"IF you love me,
you will keep my commandments."
(John 14:15)*

We *can't* love Him if we reject, deny, oppose, or reject *any* of His Word, including any of His Laws, statutes, rules, or commandments. Remember, that except for those laws which were given specifically to Israel (to separate them from all other people and nations), *all* of God's Laws and Rules were given to Mankind from a loving God in Heaven to *protect us* from the Evil One and from the terrible effects and consequences of sin.


**The Bible warns "The Falling Away," the "Rapture," The "Antichrist," and the "Apocalypse" are *all* prophetically linked together ...**

"Now brethren,
   (He is warning believing Christians)
   concerning the
   *coming of our Lord Jesus Christ*
   *and **our gathering together to Him***
   (the 'Rapture' ... the 'escape')
   Let no one deceive you by any means,
   for ***that Day***   (The Apocalypse ... *after* the Rapture)
   will not come *unless*
   ***the falling away***   (the Apostasy comes *FIRST)*
   (just like we are now seeing)
   And *the man of sin* (the coming Antichrist)
   *is revealed,* (when he *enforces* a peace upon Israel)
   the *son of perdition* (another title of the Antichrist)
   who opposes and exalts himself
   above *all* that is called God

or that is worshiped,
so that he (the coming Antichrist)
sits as God in the Temple of God,
(a new Temple *will* be built in Jerusalem)
*showing himself that he is God.*
(this event will trigger the Great Tribulation)
*Do you not remember*
*that when I was still with you*
*I told you these things?"*
(In Acts we find Paul was with them for only *3 weeks!!*)
(2 Thessalonians 2:1-5)

**This prophecy goes on to tell us the Antichrist cannot be revealed until sometime AFTER the Rapture ...**

"For the mystery of Lawlessness
  is already at work;
*Only He who now Restrains (the Holy Spirit)*
*will do so UNTIL He is taken out of the way.*
(The removal of all those filled with the Holy Spirit)
*And THEN the Antichrist ("Lawless One")*
*will be revealed,* (when he *enforces* a peace upon Israel)
whom the Lord will consume
with the breath of His mouth
and destroy with the brightness of His coming.
*The coming of the Lawless One (Antichrist)*
*is according to the working of Satan,*
*with all power, signs,* (this leader will perform *miracles*)
*and lying wonders,*
AND with all unrighteous *deception* (mixing truth with lies)
among those who perish,
*because they did NOT receive*
*the love of the truth,* (God's Word)
that they might be *saved."* (Into Heaven)
(2 Thessalonians 2:7-10)

**The Bible warns *many* deceitful teachers will successfully infiltrate into our churches ...**

"For such are false apostles,
  deceitful workers,
  (Warning: They will look and sound very Christian)
  *transforming* themselves
  into apostles of Christ.
  And no wonder!
  *For Satan himself
  transforms himself into
  an angel of light.*
  Therefore it is no great thing
  if *his* (Satan's) ministers
  *ALSO transform themselves
  into ministers of righteousness,*   (or reverends, or priests)
  whose end will be
  according to their works."
  (2 Corinthians 11:13-15)

*The "God is Love" passage will be misused to deceive many into ignoring God's Law ...*

"*Beware* of false teachers (prophets),
  who come to you in sheep's clothing,
  (they will look Christian and sound so caring)
  *but inwardly they are ravenous wolves.*"
  (Matthew 7:15)  (Leading many *away* from God's Word)

*Jesus clearly warns those who willfully and defiantly practice this (or any) form of "Lawlessness" ...*

"*NOT* everyone
  *who says to Me (Jesus), 'Lord, Lord,'
  shall enter into the Kingdom of Heaven.*
  (These people consider themselves Christians)

*MANY* ('most' or 'majority' who call themselves Christian)
will say to Me in that Day
*'Lord, Lord,* have we not *taught* (prophesied)
*in Your Name,*
cast out demons in Your Name,
and done many wonders in Your Name?
(They may have been very busy in church)
And then (at the Judgment)
I (Jesus) will declare to them
*'I never knew you,* (through love, faith, trust, and obedience)
*DEPART from Me* (out of Heaven)
*you who practice Lawlessness.'"*
(*Willfully* disobeying and ignoring God's Law)
(Matthew 7:21-23)

The *spirit* of the "Lawless One" will convince *many* to deny God's Word, or lead them to believe that times have changed and God's Rules are no longer relevant for this generation in whatever areas they wish to choose.

**A Warning to the Churches**

***Jesus warns 'lukewarm' churches (and Christians) will place their "opinions" above God's Word in the Bible ...***

"And to the angel of the church of the Laodiceans write,
 *'These things says the Amen,*
 *the Faithful and True Witness,*
 (Jesus, the Word of God, is now speaking)
 the beginning (head) of the Creation of God:
"I know your works, that you are neither cold nor hot.
I could wish you were cold or hot.
*So then, because you are LUKEWARM,*
(in love, faith, trust, and obedience to God's Word)
and neither cold nor hot,[
*I will VOMIT you out of My mouth"...*

As many as I love, I rebuke and chasten.
Therefore be zealous and repent.
*Behold, I stand at the door and knock.*
*If anyone hears My voice and opens the door,*
*I will come in to him and dine with him, and he with Me.*
To him who overcomes
I will grant to sit with Me on My throne,
as I also overcame  (at the Cross)
and sat down with My Father on His throne.
*"He who has an ear, let him hear*
*what the Spirit says to the churches."'"*
(Revelation 3:14-16,19-22)


In Greek, Laodicea can be translated "Peoples Opinions" (See below).  In John 1:1 and Revelation 19:11-14 we find Jesus Christ *is* "The Word of God."

The whole Bible, from Genesis to Revelation, is the Word of God, and we are warned in Deuteronomy and in Revelation not to add *or* take anything away from the Word of God.

We find here the Laodicean style churches have put "The Word of God" (Jesus) outside as they teach, preach, and believe their *own* "opinions" as to what is "right or wrong" and "good or evil," even if it denies, or opposes, or ignores what God's Word actually says.

We also find Jesus Christ (the Word of God), having been placed *outside* these churches, has to *knock* to get back in. We then find there are still some *individuals* in these churches who will open the door and invite Him into their lives, and with open arms and with tears of joy they will be welcomed and received into the Kingdom of Heaven.

## Churches Teaching *Opinions* and Not the Word of God

**From Moriel.org:** *The name "Laodicea" is built of a compound Greek name "lao" and "dikeaomai", meaning "people's opinions." These people and churches base their teachings and beliefs on "opinions" and not on God's Word as found in Scripture.*

## God has *also* warned us through other prophecies

"Behold, the days are coming," says the Lord GOD,
  That I will send a FAMINE on the land,
  *NOT* a famine of bread,
  *NOR* a thirst for water,
  *But of HEARING the words of the LORD."*
(Amos 8:11)

This prophecy could be somewhat analogous to a monstrous tidal wave. If we're standing on a beach and see the water rapidly start to recede from the shore we know it signifies a tidal wave is rapidly approaching which will at some point devastate and destroy everything in its path.

In our scenario, the receding water represents the teaching (and hearing) of God's Word, the shore represents our churches and synagogues, and the Tidal Wave represents the coming Apocalypse which will one day devastate and destroy almost every living thing on planet Earth. The coming Apocalypse *is* the fierce and terrible "Day of the Lord" which prophet after prophet has cried out and warned us to *watch* for and to *escape* from by drawing near to God who will lovingly hide and shelter *all* who will draw near to Him *before* "that Day."

**A Recent Voice of Warning**

One of the most popular and respected Bible teachers of the 20th Century was J. Vernon McGee who started sounding the alarm concerning the falling away ("apostasy") of the established churches over 40 years ago! Dr. McGee's warnings and writings included the following:

"We are seeing in our day an amazing, an alarming, and an awful apostasy of the church. There has always been a question among students of prophecy about just how far the organized church would go into the apostasy before the Rapture occurs.

Some of us did not believe that we would see the organized churches plunge this far into a departure from the faith before the true church — that is, the body of believers who actually trust in Christ as Savior, recognizing they are sinners and their only hope is in Him — would be taken out of the world. When Dr. William Culbertson was here in Los Angeles speaking at the Prophetic Conference, he said to some of us privately, "The things I am seeing today I thought would not take place until the Tribulation!" And I'm sure that this is the viewpoint of many students of prophecy today.

In this sense, therefore, it's an amazing apostasy that has come upon us. Suddenly the church has departed from the faith, and many of us thought that by the time this happened the true church would be gone.

It's an alarming apostasy ... and an awful apostasy. For this reason I think we can accurately say that we are right now in an amazing and alarming and awful apostasy in the church."

# HOW FAR WILL THIS GO?

## The coming "One-World" Religious System

The Bible warns around the time of the coming Apocalypse a global religion or religious system will begin to gather and rise which will draw Protestants, Roman Catholics, Islamics, Jews and other religions together through deceptive and seductive promises of "Peace" and "Love." This rising religious system will one day have a very powerful leader who will be looked upon as "a man of peace." One of this man's 33 titles found in the Bible is "the Antichrist."

The only groups who will be *excluded* from this coming One-World Religion will be Bible-believing Christians and Jews.

## The coming Antichrist will have a *RELIGIOUS* partner

"Then I saw *ANOTHER* beast
coming up out of the Earth,
and he had two horns like a lamb
and spoke like a dragon.
*And he exercises all the authority of the
first beast (the Antichrist) in his presence,
and causes the Earth and those who dwell in it
to worship the first beast (Antichrist),
whose deadly (head) wound was healed."*
(Revelation 13:11-12)

The Antichrist will not be alone. Another man, *also* empowered by Satan, will rule alongside the Antichrist. This powerful and deadly religious leader or "beast" (as God sees him) will rise to world power with the Antichrist. In this prophecy God reveals some important information and details concerning this religious man of power ...

*"Two horns like a lamb,"* tells us he will emerge with very powerful Christian credentials or doctrine, but *"Spoke like a dragon"* tells us he will be a liar and a deceiver who is controlled and directed by Satan. This person, along with the coming religious system he will lead, is also referred to in the book of Revelation as *"The Woman Who Rides the Beast."* We are warned this all-encompassing, one-world religion will rise to power out of the "City of Seven Hills" (Rome).

**This coming ecumenical Religious System will one day imprison and execute *millions* of believing Christians**

A number of years ago a Bible teacher warned that one day we would hear "ecumenical" Christians saying, "If we could just get rid of that 10% of *extremist* Christians (those "fundamentalists" who actually believe the Bible), the world would be a much better place."

**According to the Bible, these people will someday soon get their wish ...**

*The Bible-believing Christians we find below who WILL one day be imprisoned, tortured, and executed by this coming One-World Religion for their faith and trust in God's Word are those who will turn back to the Lord AFTER the Rapture, and are sometimes referred to as the "Tribulation Saints."*

**God will take the sting out of death for these millions who will die in faith, and wants them to know they will be blessed in Heaven ...**

"Then I heard a voice from Heaven
 saying to me, "Write:
 *'Blessed are the dead
 who die in the Lord from now on."* (*During* the Apocalypse)
"Yes," says the Spirit,
"that they may rest from their labors,

and their works follow them."
(Revelation 14:13)

"Then I saw the souls
of those who had been beheaded
for their witness to Jesus
and for the Word of God,
who had *not* worshiped
the beast (Antichrist) or his image,
and had *NOT* received his mark
on their foreheads or on their hands."
(Revelation 20:4)

"I saw under the altar
the souls of those who had been slain
for the Word of God
and for the testimony which they held.
And they cried with a loud voice, saying,
"How long, O Lord, holy and true,
until You judge and avenge our blood
on those who dwell on the Earth?"
*Then a white robe*
*was given to each of them;*
*and it was said to them that*
*they should rest a little while longer,*
*until both the number of their*
*fellow servants and their brethren,*
*who would be killed as they were,*
*was completed."*
(Revelation 6:9-11)

## *Jesus warns ...*

"Now brother will betray brother to death,
and a father his child;
and children will rise up against parents
and cause them to be put to death.

*"And you will be hated by all men
for My Name's sake.*
But he who *endures* to the end
*shall be saved."* (Into the Kingdom of Heaven)
(Mark 13:12-13)

Remember, one of Jesus Christ's names in the Bible is *"The Word of God"* (John 1:1 and Revelation 19:11-14). We are already starting to see people in this country and around the World being accused of "hate crimes" for simply referring to verses and passages found in the Bible, God's Word.

## Where does your church stand on Bible Prophecy?

Most churches today either reject or deny Bible Prophecy saying it's just symbolic or has already happened in the past. Others will say they refuse to teach it because "it's too divisive." Others simply ignore or avoid it because of their lack of knowledge or training in this area.

## How important *IS* Bible Prophecy in God's Word?

Overall about *25% - 30%* of the entire Bible is prophetic. Out of the 216 chapters found in the New Testament, there are *318* prophecies referencing the *Second* Coming of Christ. This represents about *one out of every thirty verses* just in the *New* Testament! Then consider that 23 out of the 27 *books* in the New Testament include prophecies. We also find that for every prophecy about Christ's first coming, there are *eight* concerning His *Second* Coming.

Yet, many of you have attended church for over 25 years and have *never* heard any detailed teachings on Bible Prophecy.

Jesus rebuked and held the religious leaders of His day accountable for *not* teaching or knowing Bible prophecies.

Many of you reading this may never have been taught and weren't even *aware* of most of the Bible prophecies found on this page, or in this book.

If a church or church leader *never* includes Bible Prophecy in their teaching, then how will the people ever know whether or not that church is one of the churches which these many prophecies concerning the Apostasy or the "falling away" are *warning* against? Or how will the people know whether we might now be drawing near to the coming Apocalypse? Or how will the people know how to *escape* (or be removed from) the coming Apocalypse in order to prepare and protect their families and children?

***For the Bible warns ...***

*"WATCH therefore, and pray ALWAYS
that you may be counted worthy to ESCAPE
all these things that will come to pass."*
(Luke 21:36)

We need to be taught and know *what things* to "Watch" for!

***Another prophetic warning to all Mankind ...***

*"Before* the decree is issued,
  *before* the day passes like chaff,
  *before* the LORD'S fierce anger comes upon you,
  *before* the Day of the LORD'S Anger comes upon you!
*Seek* the LORD,
all you meek of the Earth, who have upheld His justice.
*Seek* righteousness,
*seek* humility.
*It may be that you will be HIDDEN
in the Day of the LORD'S anger."* (The Apocalypse)
(Zephaniah 2:2-3)

God has taken *a lot* of time and effort in His Word trying to lovingly warn us of this "falling away" (Apostasy) of the churches which will trap many well-intentioned churchgoers and families unaware. God *loves* us and wants us to know the grave danger of being subtly and deceptively led away from the safety and the protection of His Word which was sent forth and given to *save us* from such things.

Yet, we will never know if we are being led astray *until* we take the time and effort to diligently study, search, and learn more of God's Word to see if these things are true.

God will never punish us for obeying His Word, as written.

Now, as you learn the Bible Prophecies you can *"Search the Scriptures daily"* to see if all these things are true.

# Time to Test

# False Prophets Would Rise

*"And many false prophets will rise and deceive many."*
*(Matthew 24:11)*

## A FALSE PROPHETS WOULD RISE AND LEAD MANY

*"And many false prophets will rise
and deceive many."
(Matthew 24:11)*

### The Bible Warns False Prophets Would Rise

The Bible warns false Prophets would rise to deceive and lead many sometime *after* the birth, death, and Resurrection of Jesus Christ.

***The Bible even specifies false prophets would one day rise with doctrines based on revelations brought by "angels" which would teach "other ways" to Heaven than the Gospel taught in the Bible ...***

"I marvel that you are turning away so soon
  from Him who called you in the grace of Christ,
to a different gospel (way to Heaven),
which is not another;
but there are some who trouble you
and want to pervert the gospel of Christ.
But even if we,
*OR AN ANGEL FROM HEAVEN,*
preach any *other* gospel to you
than what we have preached to you,
let him be accursed.
As we have said before, so now I say again,
if anyone preaches any other gospel (way to Heaven) to you
than what you have received,
let him be accursed."
(Galatians 1:6-9)

"Then if anyone says to you,
 'Look, here is the Christ (Messiah)!' or 'There!'
 do *not* believe it.
 For *false* christs and false *Prophets* will arise
 and show great signs and wonders (miracles)
 (we are warned the Antichrist *will* perform 'miracles')
 so as to deceive, if possible, even the elect.
 *See, I have told you beforehand."*
 (Meaning - "Listen up, this is a prophecy!")
"Therefore if they say to you,
 'Look, He is in the desert!'
   do not go out; or
 'Look, He is in the inner rooms!'
   do not believe it.
 *For as the lightning comes from the east
 and flashes to the west,
 so also will the coming of
 the Son of Man be."*
 (Matthew 24:23-27)

## "Or an Angel from Heaven" ...

When studying history, it is interesting to discover that both the prophet Mohammed and the prophet Joseph Smith founded their religions, Islam (Muslims) and the Church of Latter Day Saints (Mormons), on revelations which both Mohammed and Joseph Smith said were given by *angels!* Mohammed received his revelation from an angel (whom he called Gabriel) about 600 years after this Bible prophecy was written, and Joseph Smith received his revelation from an angel (he called Maroni) about 1,800 years after this prophecy was written.

It is also interesting that both religions then began to teach a different Gospel (way to Heaven) than the Bible teaches. So, in many ways Mohammed and Joseph Smith are very similar. They both said angels gave them "new" revelations because the Jews and Christians had changed the Bible. However, discoveries of the Dead Sea Scrolls, writings of the ancient church fathers, and many other ancient Bible texts prove the original Hebrew and Greek words (from which the Bible has been translated into many different languages and dialects) have not been changed (other than a few copyist errors which are well documented and do not affect any basic doctrines).

The critical issue which now separates believing Christians from Muslims and Mormons is the "Gospel" (Gospel is the Greek word for "very good news"). The Gospel promises that all who believe with a sincere "faith" that Jesus Christ willingly and lovingly suffered and died upon the Cross for all of our sins, and that He was raised from the dead on the third day, will have complete assurance all of their sins have been paid for and they will go to Heaven.

In contrast, both Muslims and Mormons are taught a different gospel which provides their followers with no assurance they will enter into Heaven after they die, for it says all people must "earn" their way into Heaven through some final balancing of the scales between their good deeds and bad deeds.

To help decide whether or not Joseph Smith or Mohammed should be categorized as false prophets from our Bible Prophecy perspective, one can also compare the prophecies found in the Old Testament (Tanakh) which were written 400-1000 years before the birth of Christ. We can find there are over 200 specific prophecies describing Messiah which Jesus fulfilled (read the *"Who IS Jesus Christ"* study), while *no* specific descriptive or detailed prophecies are found preparing the world for either Joseph Smith or Mohammed.

**The Future False Prophet**

However, the Bible does say a LOT about a yet *future* false Prophet who will one day rise, and has not yet been revealed to Mankind. Sometimes called the "Antichrist," this coming False Prophet will form a One-World Religion which will include the Roman Catholic Church, Islamics, Mormons, Buddhists, Hindus, and Protestants. We will learn much about this coming False Prophet (who will rise as a *very* popular World Leader) and his coming One-World Religion and One-World Economy in our study concerning the Antichrist.

# WARS
# &
# RUMORS OF WAR

*"Jesus answered and said to them...
'And you will hear of wars
and rumors of wars.'"
(Matthew 24:6)*

# WARS & RUMORS OF WAR

**Jesus Christ gives signs to watch for as we approach the coming Apocalypse**

"Now as He (Jesus)
   sat on the Mount of Olives (in Israel),
   the disciples came to Him privately, saying,
   *'Tell us, when will these things be?'*
   And *'What will be the sign of Your coming,
   and of the end of the Age?'"*
(Matthew 24:3)

### *Nation vs. Nation ... and ... "Ethnic" vs. "Ethnic"*

"Jesus answered and said to them . . .
   *'And you will hear of wars and rumors of wars.*
   See that you are not troubled;
   for all these things must come to pass,
   but the end is not yet.
   (Still before the Rapture and the Apocalypse)
   For nation ("ethnos") will rise against nation ("ethnos"),
   and kingdom (nation) against kingdom (nation) . . .
   All these are the *beginning* of sorrows ('birth pangs')
   (Matthew 24:6-7)

The original Greek word translated "nation" was "ethnos," from which we get our word "ethnic."

Jesus is warning we will see ethnic groups rise against ethnic groups as well as nations against nations.

**The Bible *also* tells us believing Christians are "all ONE in Christ Jesus" and there are *NO* ethnic, gender, race, or economic divisions in the "body of Christ" (Messiah)**

*"There is neither Jew nor Greek (Gentile - any non-Jew),*
  (This covers ALL races on Earth)
  *there is neither slave nor free,* (no economic divisions)
  *there is neither male nor female;* (no gender divisions)
  *for you are all one in Christ Jesus."*
(Galatians 3:28)

**The Bible warns Mankind will *never* stop war**

No world leader, no anti-war group, and no religious group (or coalition of religions) will ever bring Global Peace. God warns there will be NO peace in Israel or in the world *until* Messiah, (Jesus Christ) returns ...

**Beware of any Peace Plans for Israel!!**

"Because, even because
  they have *seduced* My people (Israel),
  saying, "Peace",
  *and there was no peace..."*
(Ezekiel 13:10)

"For they have healed the hurt
  of the daughter of My people (Israel) slightly,
  saying, 'Peace, Peace;
  *when there is no peace!"*
(Jeremiah 8:11)

"For you yourselves know perfectly
  that the Day of the Lord
  (the coming 'Apocalypse' and Armageddon)

so comes as a thief in the night.
*For when they say, 'Peace and safety!'*
*then sudden destruction comes upon them,*
as labor pains upon a pregnant woman.
*And they shall not escape."*
(1 Thessalonians 5:2-3)


## The Great Tribulation

So, although the world has always had wars, ethnic violence and strife, Jesus Christ warns that as a sign we are entering into the last days we will see these increase in frequency and size. Described as "birth pangs," these "pains" will continue to grow worse and worse, coming closer and closer together, as signs we are preparing to enter the Apocalypse.

*Jesus Christ warns . . .*

*"For then there will be Great Tribulation,*
   such as has not been
   since the beginning of the world until this time,
   no, nor ever shall be (the coming "Apocalypse").
   *And unless those days were shortened,*
   *no flesh (human being) would be saved"*
(Matthew 24:21-22)

Jesus warns that never in the history of Mankind has there *ever* been anything as terrible on Earth as the coming "Apocalypse", the "Great Tribulation", "The Day of (God's) Wrath" - the Earth will be utterly destroyed and only a small remnant of the world's population will survive.

# Time to Test

# EARTHQUAKES, FAMINES & DISEASE

*"Now as He (Jesus)
sat on the Mount of Olives,
the disciples came to Him
privately, saying,
'Tell us, when will these things be?'
And 'What will be the sign of Your coming,
and of the end of the Age?'"
(Matthew 24:3)*

## EARTHQUAKES, FAMINES & DISEASE

**Four disciples ask Jesus about the future . . .**

"Now as He (Jesus) sat on the Mount of Olives,
the disciples came to Him privately, saying,
*'Tell us, when will these things be?'*
And *'What will be the sign of Your coming,
and of the end of the Age?'"*
(Matthew 24:3)

**Here we find the sweeping scope of the prophecies Jesus is about to reveal.**

**As we study this verse, we find there will be *three* specific divisions of the future addressed:**

**1. "Tell us, when will these things be?"**

This question refers to the prophecy Jesus had just given concerning the destruction of the *Temple* (Matthew 24:2). We find the prophecies which answer this question reported and outlined in Luke's report of this prophetic discourse (Luke 19:41-44).

**2. "And what will be the sign of Your coming"**

This question refers to the signs which will be given and the events which would take place *before* He returns for His church, "As a thief in the night" (sometimes called the "Rapture"), in order to shelter and protect those who believe in Him and still wait for Him in faith from those awesome and terrible events which will strike the world during that coming period of time Jesus calls the "Great Tribulation." It is *this* portion of prophecy we are reviewing here.

## 3. "And of the end of the age?"

This question refers to the signs and events which would take place before Jesus returns the *second* time, not as a "thief in the night," but when every eye "will see the Son of Man coming on the clouds of heaven with power and great glory."

These will be the signs and events that will take place *during* that period of time Jesus calls the "Great Tribulation."

This upcoming period of time called the "Great Tribulation" is given many names in the Bible and refers to the awesome events which will take place during a 3½ year period of time which represents the last half of a very specific 7 year period of time also known as the "Apocalypse" or the prophetic 70th Week of Daniel (a week of years = 7 years. See Daniel 9:24).

The Book of Revelation (also known as the Book of the Apocalypse) lists and details the awesome and terrible events which will strike suddenly and sweep over the Earth.

## EARTHQUAKES

"Now as He (Jesus) sat on the Mount of Olives,
  the disciples came to Him privately, saying,
 'Tell us, when will these things be?'
  And 'What will be the sign of Your coming,
  and of the end of the Age?'"
  (Matthew 24:3)

"Jesus answered and said to them ...
*And there will be Earthquakes
in diverse places"*
(Matthew 24:8)

"When you *SEE*
these things, (earthquakes)
know that it is *NEAR* --
at the *DOOR!"*
(Mark 13:29)

Most people don't realize the key element to this prophecy is not just that Earthquakes will be intensifying, but the remarkable thing about this prophecy is when Jesus Christ gave this prophecy concerning the hearing of "earthquakes in diverse places" 2000 years ago, it could only be fulfilled far in the future when there would be global communication technologies such as satellite television, cell phones, and the internet capable of reporting these worldwide events as they happen.

2000 years ago the people living in Jerusalem and Israel (to whom these prophecies were first given) would never have known these earthquakes in "diverse places" had ever taken place.

So, although the world has always had Earthquakes, this Bible Prophecy tells us that as a sign we are entering into "the time of the end," we will see and hear about them almost immediately, as they increase in frequency and size.

Described as "birth pangs," these events will increase in size and frequency as signs we are preparing to enter the Apocalypse.

## FAMINES

"Now as He (Jesus) sat on the Mount of Olives,
 the disciples came to Him privately, saying,
 'Tell us, when will these things be?'
 And 'What will be the sign of Your coming,
 and of the end of the Age?'"
 (Matthew 24:3)

"Jesus answered and said to them ...

*'And there will be Famines,'*
 (Matthew 24:7)

If you do a study of Famines today, you will find famines often follow war (remember Jesus had also just predicted "Wars and rumors of War" leading up to the coming Apocalypse in this same prophetic passage). Today, most famines are man-made. Stalin's Communist (Socialist) controlled Russia murdered hundreds of thousands of men, women, and children using a man-made famine, and around the world today we can find famines being used as a weapon by one political, religious, or ethnic group against another.

## DEADLY DISEASES SPREADING

"Now as He (Jesus Christ) sat on the Mount of Olives,
 the disciples came to Him privately, saying,
 'Tell us, when will these things be?'
 And 'What will be the sign of Your coming,
 and of the end of the Age?'"
 (Matthew 24:3)

"Jesus answered and said to them ...
 'And there will be
 *Deadly diseases (pestilence) spreading'*
 (Matthew 24:7)

Study the news to see the frightening number of new drug resistant, mosquito-borne, and incurable sexually transmitted diseases which are now spreading rapidly around the world.

Just as with the earthquake prophecy, these prophecies concerning famines and deadly diseases are also remarkable because these Bible Prophecies could only be fulfilled with global communication technologies capable of reporting these things on a world wide scale (see the prophecies concerning 'Travel and Knowledge' increasing).

Even though the world has always had famines, diseases, and earthquakes, the Bible warns us that as a sign we are entering into 'the time of the end' we will see these things increase in frequency.

Described as "birth pangs," these pains will continue to grow worse and worse, coming closer and closer together, as signs we are preparing to enter into the time of the coming 7 year Apocalypse.

For this same Bible Prophecy which was given concerning these earthquakes, famines, and deadly diseases also goes on to warn ..

"For then there will be Great Tribulation,
　　such as has not been
　　since the beginning of the world until this time,
　　no, nor ever shall be (the coming "Apocalypse").
　　*And unless those days were shortened,*
　　*no human being (flesh) would be saved"*
(Matthew 24:21-22)

The Bible warns here that *never* in the history of Mankind has there been anything as terrible on Earth as the coming Apocalypse (called here the "Great Tribulation"), when only a small remnant of the world will survive.

# KNOWLEDGE & TRAVEL WILL INCREASE AT "THE TIME OF THE END"

*"But you, Daniel,
shut up the words,
and seal the book
UNTIL the Time of the End.
Many shall run to and fro,
and knowledge shall increase."
(Daniel 12:4)*

# KNOWLEDGE & TRAVEL WILL INCREASE AT "THE TIME OF THE END"

"But you, Daniel,
shut up the words,
and seal the book
*UNTIL the Time of the End.
Many shall run to and fro,
and knowledge shall increase.*"
(Daniel 12:4)

This is an interesting Bible prophecy. This prophecy (written around 2,500 years ago) warns that around *"The time of the end"* both travel (running to a fro) *and* knowledge would begin to increase at a rate unlike anything ever seen in the history of Mankind.

**A remarkable Bible prophecy from the book of Daniel ...**

"But you, Daniel,
 shut up the words,
 and seal the book
 *UNTIL the time of the end.*
 Many shall *travel* (run to and fro)
 *and knowledge shall increase.*"
(Daniel 12:4)

Daniel the prophet (book of Daniel) received some of the most sweeping prophecies found in the Bible. Prophecies found in the book of Daniel take us from the days of the Babylonian captivity to the exact day on which Messiah would be revealed, and on to the very end of this Age.

It is fascinating to see how God told Daniel (after giving him some of the most remarkable prophecies found in the Bible), to "Shut up the words and seal the book *UNTIL the time of the end"* and then gives Daniel (and us) two signs that would help Mankind *identify* "The time of the end."

### #1. Travel:
The ability to travel from one place to another would be unlike anything seen before in history, and the vast numbers of people traveling all over the globe would be unprecedented.

It is interesting to note from the time Daniel wrote this Bible Prophecy until just around the 20th century, the speed at which man could travel remained fairly constant and was limited to the speed of foot, horse, and sailboat. Mankind then moved quickly from riding horseback to landing on the Moon in a very short period of time.

If you have any questions as to whether or not we are seeing the fulfillment of this prophecy, just look at the non-stop *air* traffic all around the globe (which fulfills both the travel and knowledge portions of this prophecy), and consider the vast number of commuters and travelers now using our freeways, roads, and highways on a daily basis.

What we are now seeing today has no equal in the annals of history.

### #2. Knowledge:
Knowledge would increase at a rate unlike any other time in history.

Do an Internet search on how long it now takes the sum total of Man's knowledge to double. It is interesting how many reports and articles report the sum total of Man's knowledge is now doubling at a rate unlike anything ever seen in the history of Mankind. Many colleges and universities have now been forced to use on-line digital textbooks which can be continually updated, because the rate of change has increased so rapidly that printed textbooks have a difficult time keeping current with all of the new technologies, products, and procedures being introduced into all fields, and not just limited to science, medicine, and industry.

# Time to Test

# GLOBAL WEATHER EXTREMES

*"Have you entered the treasury of snow,*
*Or have you seen the treasury of hail,*
*Which I (God) have reserved*
*For the Time of Trouble (Tribulation),*
*For the Day of Battle and War?"*
*(Job 38:22-23)*

## PROPHETIC WEATHER FORECAST FOR PLANET EARTH

*"Have you entered the treasury of snow,*
*Or have you seen the treasury of hail,*
*Which I (God) have reserved*
*For the Time of Trouble (Tribulation),*
*For the Day of Battle and War?"*
(Job 38:22-23)

**The Bible warns of global weather extremes with great atmospheric upheaval around the time of the coming Apocalypse ...**

- **Extreme Frost and Snow**
- **Huge and Deadly Hail Storms**
- **Heat From the Sun Will Scorch the Earth**
- **Exceedingly Great Storms and Hurricanes**

Both cataclysmic global cooling *and* global warming lie ahead for all who are left on Earth after the coming "Rapture" (which will be reviewed in a later chapter).

### There will be a great plague of *snow* coming upon the Earth

"Have you entered the treasury of snow,
 Or have you seen the treasury of hail,
 Which I (God) have reserved
 *for the Time of Trouble (Tribulation),*
 *For the Day of battle and war?"* (The coming Apocalypse)
(Job 38:22-23)

## There will be a great plague of *hail* coming upon the Earth

*"And great hail from heaven*
*fell upon men,* ("mankind".. men and women)
each hailstone about the weight of a talent.
(A "talent" ≈ 85 - 114 pounds!!)
Men blasphemed God because of the plague of the hail,
since that plague was exceedingly great."
(Revelation 16:21)

It's interesting to note that chronologically speaking, many believe the book of Job and the book of Revelation were the first and the last books written in the Bible.


## A great heat from *the Sun* will scorch the people on Earth

*"Then the fourth angel poured out his bowl on the Sun,*
   and power was given to him to scorch men with fire.
   *And men were scorched with great heat,*
   and they blasphemed the Name of God
   who has power over these plagues;
   and they did not repent and give Him glory."
(Revelation 16:8-9)


In studying Bible Prophecies, it appears any global "Climate Plans" trying to legislate or control global warming will be just as fruitless as trying to eliminate wars (or diseases) any time before the coming "Time of the end."

**An ancient Bible Prophecy even gives us an accurate *Environmental* forecast for planet Earth around the time of the coming Apocalypse ...**

"*The Earth will wear out (grow old) like a garment,*
  And those who dwell in it will die in like manner;
  But My (God's) salvation will be forever,
  And My righteousness will not be abolished."
(Isaiah 51:6)

**There will be unimaginable and exceedingly great storms and hurricanes**

"And there will be signs
  in the Sun, in the Moon,
  and in the Stars;
  and, on the Earth
  distress of nations, with perplexity,
  *the sea and the waves roaring*"
(Luke 21:25)


The record cold and the record hot temperatures, along with the record draughts, and the record rainfalls that we have been seeing over these past few years are *not* man made, they are *God* made, and are given to us as warning signs that global weather extremes *which will be far worse than what we are seeing* now lie ahead.

# Russia

# Iran

# and

# Allies

*"In the latter years
you will come into the land
of those brought back from the sword
and gathered from many people
on the mountains of Israel,
which had long been desolate
they were brought out of the nations,
and now all of them dwell safely.
You will ascend, coming like a storm,
covering the land (of Israel) like a cloud,
you and all your troops
and many peoples with you."
(Ezekiel 38:8-10)*

# RUSSIA, IRAN AND ALLIES WILL INVADE ISRAEL

## A Prophetic War of the Ages

### Ezekiel 38

THIS WAR will be unlike any other war in history.

This war will unleash a series of *irreversible* events which will change the world ... *forever!*

God has set aside two whole chapters in the Bible to warn Mankind of this coming war.

The Bible warns Russia, Iran, Turkey, and a coalition of nations will go to war and *will* invade Israel. In Ezekiel 38-39 the Bible warns this coming war between Russia, Iran, and Israel will take place sometime after Israel has been re-gathered into Her land as a nation (which was fulfilled on May 14, 1948).

*This prophetic war has never yet taken place.*

The only time in history Iran (Persia) has ever gone to war against Israel was to *help* Israel throw off the yoke of the Byzantine Empire around 614 AD.

THE BIBLE warns the US will *NOT* defend Israel. According to the Bible, Israel must stand alone ... *with God.* For when this coming war does finally start, the United States will be unwilling (or unable) to help Israel defend herself. Even though the Bible warns the invading armies will be ultimately destroyed by God, it will be a devastating war for both Israel and the whole world.

Bible scholars are divided as to whether this coming war is part of the prophetic battle of Armageddon or will just precede Armageddon in order to prepare a path for the Antichrist (a coming World Leader who will enforce a Peace Plan ("covenant") upon Israel) which will trigger the final prophetic 7-Year period of time which God has set aside for Israel and the World which is sometimes called the "Apocalypse" ...

ALL MANKIND should be sitting on the edge of their seats with white knuckles watching this terrible prophecy slowly start to unfold ...

### Ezekiel 38:1-10

"Now the Word of the LORD came to me, saying,
'Son of man,
  set your face against Gog (a powerful leader),
  of the land of Magog, (*Russia!*)
  (Magog in Hebrew is "Scythia" in Greek)
  the prince of Rosh, Meshech, and Tubal,
  (Meshech and Tubal are in and around Turkey)
  and prophesy against him (Gog), and say,
  Thus says the Lord GOD:
'Behold, I (God) am against you, O Gog
  (Powerful human *or* angelic-demonic ruler)
  the prince of Rosh,
  Meshech, and Tubal. *(Turkey!)*
  I (God) will turn you (Russia) around,
  *put hooks into your jaws,*
  (Israel's "Leviathan" gas fields may be the "bait")
  and lead you out,
  with all your army,
  horses, and horsemen,
  all splendidly clothed,
  a great company with bucklers and shields,

*All* of them handling swords (weapons).
(Russia will form a powerful coalition)
*Iran* (Persia),   (Iran is listed first as the lead ally)
*Sudan* ("Cush" - often translated 'Ethiopia'),
and *Libya* (northern Africa)
are with them,
*all* of them with shield and helmet.
*Germany* (Gomer - also possibly 'Galatia' Turkey)
and all its troops;
*Armenia* (the house of Togarmah)
from the far north and all its troops -
*many* people are with you."
(Ezekiel 38:1-6)


**The Bible warns Russia will act as a GUARD for Iran and their allies ...**

"Prepare yourself  (Russia - "Magog")
 and be ready,
 you (Russia)
 and all your companies (allies)
 that are gathered about you;
 and be a GUARD for them."
 ("Them" is Iran, Turkey, and the other allies listed)
(Ezekiel 38:7)

A "guard" protects, defends, blocks threats of "international sanctions"... and provides weapons, technology, intelligence, command, and control ... and often stays quietly hidden in the shadows until the time is right.

**This prophetic war must take place AFTER Israel was re-gathered in her Land (1948) ...**

"*After many days* you will be visited.
  (This war would happen far from Ezekiel's time)

In the latter years you (Russia-Iran-Turkey)
will come into the land of those
brought back from the sword *(Israel!)*
and gathered from many people
on the mountains of Israel,
which had long been desolate
(This war has to happen *after* 1948)
they (the children of Israel)
were brought out of the nations, (Plural, *not* Babylon)
and now all of them dwell safely.
*You will ascend, coming like a storm,*
*covering the land (of Israel) like a cloud,*
*(Bombers, fighter-jets, massive missile barrages?)*
*you and all your troops and many peoples with you."*
(Ezekiel 38:8-10)


## *Ezekiel 38:11-17 ...*

*"Thus says the Lord GOD:*
"On that Day it shall come to pass
 that thoughts will arise in your mind,
 and you will make an evil plan:
 You (the one who leads Russia) will say,
 'I will go up against a land of unwalled villages;
 (Cities in Israel are no longer 'walled')
 I will go to a peaceful people, who dwell safely,
 all of them dwelling without walls,
 and having neither bars nor gates'
 to take plunder and to take booty,
 (Greed, envy, and arrogance will fuel this invasion)
 to stretch out your hand against the waste places
 that are again inhabited, (look at Israel today)
 and against a people gathered from the nations,
 (this must take place *after* 1948!)
 who have acquired livestock and goods,
 who dwell in the midst of the land.

Sheba (Saudi Arabia), Dedan (Kuwait),
(Saudi Arabia will *not* join this invasion)
the merchants of Tarshish (may be England),
and all their young lions
(may be former colonies like Canada, Australia, US)
will say to you,
'Have you come to take plunder?
(Greed, envy, and arrogance will fuel this invasion)
Have you gathered your army to take booty,
to carry away silver and gold,
to take away livestock and goods,
to take great plunder?'"
*"Therefore, son of man,*
*prophesy, and say to Gog,*
Thus says the Lord God:
On that Day when My people Israel
are dwelling securely,
will you not know it?
You will come from your place
OUT OF THE UTTERMOST PARTS
OF THE NORTH,
(Russia now claims the Arctic *and* the North Pole)
you and many peoples with you,
all of them riding on horses,
a great host, a mighty army.
You will come up against
*My people Israel,* (not a good idea)
like a cloud covering the Land.
*In the latter days*
(Which we are now in)
I will bring you against *My* Land,
(God says Israel is His Land)
that the nations may know Me,
when through you, O Gog,
I vindicate My Holiness before their eyes."
(*God* will destroy this invading army)

Thus says the Lord GOD:
"Are you (Gog) he of whom
I have spoken in former days   (Prophecy fulfilled!)
by My servants the prophets of Israel,
who prophesied for years in those days
that I (God) would bring you against them?"
(Ezekiel 38:11-17)

## *Ezekiel 38:18-23 ...*

"And it will come to pass
  at the same time, when Gog
  comes against the land of Israel," says the Lord GOD,
"that My (God's) fury will show in My face.
  For in My jealousy and
  in the fire of My wrath
  I have spoken:
'Surely in that day
  there shall be a great earthquake
  in the land of Israel,
  so that the fish of the sea,
  the birds of the heavens,
  the beasts of the field,
  all creeping things
  that creep on the earth,
  and all men who are on the face of the Earth
  shall shake at My presence.
  The mountains shall be thrown down,
  the steep places shall fall,
  and every wall shall fall to the ground.'
  I will call for a sword against Gog
  throughout all My mountains,"
  says the Lord GOD.
*"Every man's sword will be against his brother.*
  (These armies will turn against each other)
  And I will bring him to judgment
  with pestilence and bloodshed;

I will rain down on him, on his troops,
and on the many peoples who are with him,
flooding rain, great hailstones, fire, and brimstone.
(These armies will be destroyed by God!)
Thus I (God) will magnify Myself
and sanctify Myself,
and I will be known
in the eyes of many nations.
*Then they shall know
that I AM the LORD."'*
(Ezekiel 38:18-23)

We are not exactly sure when this attack/invasion will take place. But, from current news headlines, it looks as though it is now getting very close. As noted above, if you study your history books you will find the only time in history Iran (Persia) has invaded Israel was in 614 AD, and this invasion was to help Israel break the yoke of the Byzantine Empire. The current threats of war Iran is making against Israel represent the first time in history the world has seen the imminent fulfillment of this prophecy. Add the fact Russia is fully backing Iran, and Turkey has now turned toward Russia and against Israel, and all of these nations either are, or soon will be, armed with nuclear weapons, you will find the world may soon be facing this terrible prophetic war.

### *Where is Syria?*

It is notable that *Syria* (or its ancient name Aram) is *not* listed among the Russia-Iran coalition of allies. It may be the prophecy concerning the total destruction of Damascus will be fulfilled just prior to this invasion.

### *The invading armies will be utterly destroyed by GOD!!!*

As we will see in the next chapter the Bible goes on to warn the invading armies will be utterly destroyed ... *by GOD!*

Some scholars feel this coming war must be part of, or the beginning of "The Battle of Armageddon" (because of some of the terminology used), and others believe it must happen sometime before Armageddon and will set the stage for the coming "Antichrist" (who will rise over 10 nations which were part of the Roman Empire) to fill the world power vacuum that will be left after this coming war ...

## *The United States will be "neutralized"*

The United States will be "neutralized" (either politically, economically, militarily, or all of the above) sometime *before* this attack and will be unwilling or unable to help defend Israel, for the Bible warns Israel must stand alone ... *with God!*

More importantly, many good Bible prophecy scholars believe the strange prophetic event called "The Rapture" must take place sometime before God intervenes in this coming battle.

## *Please do not ignore these Bible prophecies.*

Many people will simply yawn and ignore these Bible prophecies and the headlines we are now seeing.

Yet, God does *not* fulfill His prophecies or prophetic warnings in secret, but so all the world can see. For many years now a number of Bible prophecy teachers and scholars have been warning the one piece of the puzzle missing was for Turkey (a NATO ally-nation) to turn toward Russia and Iran and against Israel (as this prophecy predicts, and we are now seeing.)

The world has waited over 2,500 years to see the headlines we are now seeing. God expects us to take His prophetic warnings seriously, and not to ignore, mock, or reject them.

# The Invading Armies Will Be Destroyed

> *"Thus says the Lord God:*
> *"Behold, I am against you, O Gog...*
> *and I will turn you around*
> *and lead you on, bringing you up*
> *from the uttermost parts of the North*
> *and bring you against*
> *the mountains of Israel.*
> *You shall fall upon the mountains of Israel,*
> *you and all your troops...*
> *You shall fall on the open field;*
> *for I have spoken,'*
> *says the Lord God".*
> *(Ezekiel 39:1,2,4)*

## GOD WILL INTERVENE FOR ISRAEL

**Ezekiel 39**

As we will see in this chapter the Bible goes on to warn the invading armies will be utterly destroyed ... *by GOD!*

Here in Ezekiel 39 we will also find hints this coming war may go nuclear because Israel will wait months to enter the battlefield after the battle, they will "set apart men regularly employed" (professionals) to bury the dead, and later if a bone is spotted it is to be "marked" for the professionals to bury (exactly the same procedures that are now found in our military nuclear/biological/chemical "battlefield cleanup" manuals today) ... the aftermath of this invasion will be very, very gruesome.

***The invading armies will be utterly destroyed by GOD!!!***

"And you, son of man,
  prophesy against Gog, and say,
'Thus says the Lord God:
"Behold, I am against you, O Gog,
 (Gog is either the human or a powerful angelic ruler)
  the prince of Rosh, Meshech, and Tubal;
  and I will turn you around and lead you on,
  bringing you up from
  THE UTTER PARTS OF THE NORTH,
  (Look at a map from Israel)
  (Russia's army now claims the Arctic *and* the North Pole)
  and bring you against the mountains of Israel.
  *Then I (God) will knock the bow out of your left hand,
  and cause the arrows to fall out of your right hand.
  You shall fall upon the mountains of Israel,
  you and all your troops*

*and the peoples who are with you;*
I will give you to birds of prey of every sort
and to the beasts of the field to be devoured.
You shall fall on the open field;
for I have spoken," says the Lord God.
*"And I will send fire on Magog*
*and on those who live in security*
*in the coastlands.* (Massive nuclear exchange?)
Then they shall *know*
that I am the Lord.
So I will make My Holy Name known
in the midst of My people Israel,
and I will not let them profane
My Holy Name anymore. (See Ezekiel 36:17-23)
Then the *nations* shall know
*that I am the Lord*, (the whole world will know it is God)
the Holy One in Israel.
*Surely it is coming,*
*and it shall be done,"*
*says the Lord God.*
"This is the Day of which I have spoken.
"Then those who dwell in the cities of Israel
 will go out and set on fire
 and burn the weapons,
 both the shields and bucklers,
 the bows and arrows,
 the javelins and spears;
 and they will make fires with them
 for seven years. (From nuclear warheads?)
 They will not take wood from the field
 nor cut down any from the forests,
 *because they will make fires with the weapons;*
 and they will plunder those who plundered them,
 and pillage those who pillaged them,"
 says the Lord God.
 (Ezekiel 39:1-10)

### *Now, some interesting Battlefield Cleanup details ...*

"It will come to pass in that Day
that I will give Gog a burial place there in Israel,
the valley of those who pass by east of the sea;
and it will obstruct travelers,
because there they will bury Gog
and all his multitude.
Therefore they will call it
the Valley of Hamon Gog. (Means multitude of Gog)
*For seven months*
*the house of Israel will be burying them,*
*in order to cleanse the land.*
Indeed all the people of the land will be burying,
and they will gain renown for it
on the day that I am glorified," says the Lord God.
*"They will set apart men regularly employed,* (Professionals)
*with the help of a search party,*
*to pass through the land*
*and bury those bodies remaining on the ground,*
*in order to cleanse it.*
At the *end* of seven months
they will make a search.
The search party will pass through the land;
*and when anyone sees a man's bone,*
*he shall set up a marker by it,*
*till the buriers have buried it*
(Very similar to Nuclear-Biological-Chemical procedures)
in the Valley of Hamon Gog.
The name of the city will also be Hamonah.
Thus they shall cleanse the land.'"
(Ezekiel 39:11-16)

## Israel will be restored to the Land ... *and* to God

*"I will set My glory among the nations;*
*ALL the nations shall see My judgment*
*which I have executed,*
and My hand which I have laid on them.
So the house of Israel shall know
*that I am the Lord their God*
*from that day forward.*
(The Rapture should take place *before* God intervenes.)
The *Gentiles* shall know
that the house of Israel
went into captivity for their iniquity;
*because they were unfaithful to Me,*
therefore I hid My face from them.
I gave them into the hand of their enemies,
and they all fell by the sword.
*According to their uncleanness*
*and according to their transgressions*
*I have dealt with them,*
*and hidden My face from them."'*

"Therefore thus says the Lord God:
'*Now* I will bring back the captives of Jacob,
*and have mercy on the whole house of Israel;*
and I will be jealous for My Holy Name - -
*after* they have borne their shame,
(This will be a *terrible* time for Israel *and* the world)
and all their unfaithfulness
in which they were unfaithful to Me,
when they dwelt safely in their own land
and no one made them afraid.
When I have brought them back from the peoples
and gathered them out of their enemies' lands,
and I am hallowed in them
in the sight of many nations,

then they shall know that I am the Lord their God,
who sent them into captivity among the nations,
but also brought them back to their land,
and left none of them captive any longer.
*And I will not hide My face from them anymore;
for I shall have poured out My Spirit
on the house of Israel,' says the Lord God."*
(Ezekiel 39:21-29)

This coming war will be a War of the Ages. This is why many Bible scholars are divided as to whether or not these verses reflect the coming Battle of Armageddon. But, most (not all) agree the Rapture must take place sometime *before* God intervenes for Israel against Russia-Iran and their allies, which shows the time-frame as either in or just before the "70th Week of Daniel" (the 7 Year Apocalypse) when God has removed all the believing Christians from the Earth to then focus specifically on (and through) *Israel.*

**One Bible teacher described Armageddon as the WAR of Armageddon which will have 3 phases:**

**First:**
The Russia-Iran-Turkey and allies war where specific coalition nations are listed, while many nations (including Saudi Arabia and Egypt) are conspicuously absent from this list of nations coming against Israel. Also, this war is ignited through greed and "taking spoils" (the massive Israeli Leviathan oil/gas fields?)

**Second:**
When the "kings of the East" (China and allies) with a massive 200,000,000 army will invade the Middle-East and unleash their weapons of mass destruction, quickly killing 1/3 of all Mankind. This we are told will draw the attention of the Antichrist (and coming world leader) who will respond (see the book of Revelation chapters 9 and 16).

**Third:**

When ALL the armies of the world will gather together under the leadership of the coming Antichrist to invade Israel from the west, east, north, and south to take *Jerusalem.*

The prophecy of Enoch which we will review in the next chapter seems to confirm the coming Battle of Armageddon (when the armies converge from all directions, and not just the "utter parts of the north") will take place sometime *after* the Russia-Iran invasion.

However, it's interesting because Enoch spends much more time detailing the apparent Russia-Iran invasion of Israel than he does the final Battle of Armageddon invasion.

It appears (and I could be wrong) that this coming Russia, Iran, Turkey, and allies war against Israel will trigger a series of irreversible events ending with the final Battle of Armageddon which will climax the end of all human history as we know it.

# By Two or Three Witnesses

*"In the mouths of 2 or 3 witnesses shall a thing be established."*
*(Deuteronomy 17:6 & 2 Corinthians 13:1)*

## BY TWO OR THREE WITNESSES

### The Book of Ezekiel
### *AND*
### The Book of Enoch

*"In the mouths of 2 or 3 witnesses
shall a thing be established."*
(Deuteronomy 17:6 & 2 Corinthians 13:1)

The books of Ezekiel and the book of Enoch *both* warn of a prophetic Russia-Iran war against Israel which will trigger an *irreversible* series of events which will lead to the Battle of Armageddon (and the end of this Age.)

Note: The book of Enoch is an ancient book (Enoch was Noah's great-grandfather), and portions of at least 10 copies of the book were found among the Dead Sea Scrolls.

Although the book of Enoch is relatively unknown because it is in disfavor with many churches today for its detailed description of angelic interactions with mankind, many of the early church fathers such as Justin Martyr, Tatian, Irenaeus, Bishop of Lyons, Clement of Alexandria, Tertullian, Origen, Methodius of Philippi, and Ambrose of Milan also accepted the book of Enoch as Scriptural writing.

The ancient Ethiopian Church and the Coptic Church in Egypt have always accepted it as Biblical canon. Another prophecy from Enoch is found quoted directly in the book of Jude in the New Testament (Jude 1:14-15).

# From The Book of Enoch 1

## Enoch 1: 2nd Book of Parables

"And in those days, the Angels will gather together, and will throw themselves towards the east, upon the Parthians (an ancient empire which included Iran-Persia which was founded by a Russian-Scythian) and Medes.

They will stir up the kings so that a disturbing spirit will come upon them, and they will drive them from their thrones; and they will come out like lions from their lairs, and like hungry wolves in the middle of their flocks.

56.6 And they will go up and trample on the Land of My Chosen Ones (Israel), and the land of My chosen ones will become before them a tramping-ground and a beaten track.

56.7 But the City of My Righteous Ones (Jerusalem) will be a hindrance to their horses, and they will stir up slaughter amongst themselves (God will turn this invading army against themselves), and their own right hand will be strong against them.

And a man will not admit to knowing his neighbor, or his brother, nor a son his father, or his mother, until, through their death, there are corpses enough; and their punishment - it will not be in vain. And in those days Sheol (Hell) will open its mouth and they will sink into it and their destruction; Sheol will swallow up the sinners in front of the faces of the Chosen."

57.1 And it came to pass, AFTER this that I saw *another* host of chariots with men riding on them, and they came upon the wind *from the east and from the west, to the south.* (The prophecies of Armageddon in Revelation also describe a global East-West-South gathering of the *world's* armies in Israel.)

57.2 And the sound of the noise of their chariots was heard. And when this occurred the Holy Ones observed it from Heaven *and the Pillars of the Earth were shaken from their foundations.*

*And the sound was heard from the ends of the Earth to the ends of Heaven throughout one day.* (Armageddon!!)

And all will fall down and worship the Lord of Spirits

And this is the end of the second parable."

Note: This prophecy takes us to the very end of the Age of Mankind, just before final Battle of Armageddon. This ancient prophecy may act as an independent "second witness" confirming the prophetic significance of this coming prophetic war found written in the book of Ezekiel.

It appears from this prophecy that the final Battle of Armageddon (which will be fought over *Jerusalem* and not over "spoils"), will take place sometime fairly soon *after* the Russia-Iran invasion of Israel.

## The Identity of "Russia - Magog - Scythia"

Note: "One of the earliest references to Magog was by Hesiod, "the father of Greek didactic poetry," who identified Magog with the Scythians and southern Russia in the 7th century B.C."

Note: "Strabo (xi, 515) says the first Parthian (Arsaces) was a SCYTHIAN"   (www.parthia.com)

From the Roman-Jewish historian Josephus Flavius
A major source on ancient Jewish-Roman history is Josephus Flavius, a Jewish-Roman historian who wrote of the Roman wars and witnessed the Roman siege on Jerusalem in 70 A.D. Josephus identified Magog in his ancient writings as he wrote ... "Magog founded the Magogians, thus named after him, but who were by the Greeks called 'Scythians.'"   (Josephus, Antiquities, 1.123)

From the Wikipedia Encyclopedia - Scythia (Magog in Hebrew) comprised an area in Eurasia inhabited in ancient times by Iranian nomadic peoples, speaking Iranian languages and known as the Scythians or Scyths. The location and extent of Scythia varied over time, from the Altay Mountains region where Mongolia, China, Russia, and Kazakhstan come together, across southern Ukraine to the lower Danube river area, Bulgaria and Georgia. The Chinese knew the Saka (Asian Scythians) as Sai. The Scythians first appear in Assyrian annals as Ishkuzai, reported as pouring in from the north some time around 700 BC and settling in

Ascania and modern Azerbaijan as far as to the southeast of Lake Urmia. Archaeological remains of the Scythians include elaborate tombs containing gold, silk, horses and human sacrifices. Mummification techniques and permafrost have aided in the relative preservation of some remains.

From 'Encyclopedia.com - Scythia (Magog in Hebrew), ancient region of Eurasia, extending from the Danube river on the west to the borders of China on the east. The Scythians flourished from the 8th to the 4th cent. BC They spoke an Indo-Iranian language but had no system of writing. They were nomadic conquerors and skilled horsemen. They seem to be related to the Saka, another nomadic tribe that roamed the steppes of central Asia at about the same time. The so-called Royal Scyths established a kingdom in the E Crimea before the 9th cent. BC They seem to have maintained themselves as a ruling class while others (probably native inhabitants) worked the grain fields. The Scythians are traditionally associated with the area between the Danube and the Don, but modern excavations in the Altai Mts., particularly at the site of Pazyryk, suggest that their origins were in Western Siberia (Russia) before they moved east into Southern Russia in the early 1st millennium BC. Scythian power was maintained in the 8th cent. BC in obscure warfare with the Cimmerians. In South Russia they were displaced (2nd or 1st century BC) by the related Sarmatians.

From Chuck Missler's 'Koinonia House' Article - Magog-Scythia (http://www.khouse.org/articles/2002/427/)

We know the descendants of Magog by their Greek designation as the Scythians (depicted in their legends as descending from Scythes, the youngest of the three sons of Heracles, from sleeping with a half viper and half woman).

The name Scythian designates a number of nomadic tribes from the Russian steppes, one group of which invaded the Near East in the 8th and 7th centuries B.C. After being repulsed from Media, many of the later Scyths settled in the fertile area of the Ukraine north of the Black Sea. Other related tribes occupied the area to the east of the Caspian Sea.

The ancient Greek historian Herodotus (5th century B.C) describes them living in Scythia (i.e., the territory north of the Black Sea). He describes Scythia as a square, 20 days journey (360 miles) on a side. It encompassed the lower reaches of the Dniester, Bug, Dnieper, and Don Rivers where they flow into the Black Sea and the Sea of Azov.

The Scythian language belonged to the Iranian family of the Indo-European languages. The Ossetian dialect of central Caucasus appears to be a survivor. The original area in which Iranian was spoken extended from the mid-Volga and the Don regions to the northern Urals and beyond. From here, Iranian-speaking tribes colonized Media, Parthia, Persia, Central Asia, and as far as the Chinese border.

In the 7th century B.C. the Scythians swept across the area, displacing the Cimmerians from the steppes of the Ukraine east of Dnieper River, who fled from them across the Caucasus. It is provocative that even the name "Caucasus" appears to have been derived from Gog-hasan, or "Gog's Fort."

# Bible Prophecy of Syria

*"Behold, Damascus is taken away from being a city, and it shall be a ruinous heap" (Isaiah 17:1)*

## Prophecy of Syria

*"Behold,
Damascus is taken away
from being a city,
and it shall be
a ruinous heap"
(Isaiah 17:1)*

***Bible Prophecy warns Damascus will be utterly destroyed ...***

Many historians believe Damascus may be the oldest continually inhabited city in the world, and there is no record in ancient history of it ever being fully destroyed. Syria is almost a 'city-state' with much of its population living in and around the city of Damascus.

Syria, like the rest of Israel's Islamic neighbors hates Israel and has publicly called for the destruction of Israel. Syria has also, for the first time in history, recently formed a strategic military alliance with both Russia and Iran, with their armies currently taking up battle positions along Syria's border with Israel.

Turkey has also recently formed a military alliance with Russia and is holding high-level military cooperation meetings with Iran. An article from Israel recently reported Iran now has at least 13 permanent military bases in Syria.

It is interesting to note in the 1973 Yom Kippur war Israel considered using nuclear weapons against their enemies when early in the war it appeared Israel would be overrun and defeated by the invading Islamic armies.

***Damascus, Syria will someday be utterly destroyed, and will become "a ruinous heap"* ...**

"The burden of Damascus.
Behold,
*Damascus is taken away
from being a city,
and it shall be
a ruinous heap"*
(Isaiah 17:1)

***This prophecy has never yet been fulfilled* ...**

This prophecy has never yet been fulfilled. It is also notable that Syria (or its ancient name Aram) is not listed among the Russia-Iran allies which will attack and invade Israel in Ezekiel 38. It may be this prophecy concerning the destruction of Damascus will be fulfilled just prior to the Russia-Iran invasion, or could even possibly be the catalyst for this coming Russia-Iran invasion of Israel.

The Bible then goes on to warn this prophecy will be fulfilled during a time of *great trouble* for nation Israel ...

"And in that Day it shall come to pass,
the glory of Jacob (Israel)
shall be made thin,
and the fatness of his flesh shall wax lean."
(Isaiah 17:4)

There will be a coming time of trouble unlike anything in the history of the nation coming to the land of Israel. Jeremiah calls it "The Time of Jacob's (Israel's) Trouble" (Jeremiah 30:7). It is hard to tell if this happens after Damascus is destroyed, or at the same time.

We do know from Bible prophecies there will be a coming 3 1/2 year period of false peace in Israel brought in by a strong, powerful, and very popular world leader (also called the "Antichrist") who will someday enforce a covenant or 'peace plan' upon nation Israel which will mark the exact beginning of the coming 7-year "Apocalypse."

We are told here (and in other prophetic passages) that a remnant in Israel will turn back to God and His Word around the time of Armageddon as they come to believe, from Scripture, that Jesus Christ (Yeshua Ha'Mashiach in Hebrew), is the Eternal One ("from of old, from everlasting" see Micah 5:2), the Messiah and Holy One of Israel ...

"At that Day shall a man
 look to his Maker,
 and his eyes shall have respect
 to the Holy One (Messiah) of Israel."
(Isaiah 17:7)

*God tells us WHY Jacob's (Israel's) "Trouble" will come ...*

*"Because thou hast forgotten
 the God of thy Salvation,
 and hast not been mindful
 of the Rock of thy strength."* (Messiah!)
(Isaiah 17:10)

As mentioned earlier, it is notable that *Syria* (or its ancient name Aram) is *not* listed among the Russia-Iran coalition of allies. It may be the prophecy concerning the total destruction of Damascus will be fulfilled just prior to this invasion. In fact, it's possible that this attack against Syria may prompt the Russia, Iran & allies invasion of Israel.

# Time to Test

## PROPHECIES OF SYRIA
## from
## EZRA 2

The ancient book called *The Apocalypse of Ezra* or *2 Esdras (Ezra)* includes some very interesting and specific (and possibly timely) prophecies concerning Syria, Russia, and Iran in the last days, or the end times.

The *Apocalypse of Ezra,* which is also sometimes called the *Jewish Apocalypse of Ezra,* is said to have been written by the same author who wrote the book of Ezra found in the Bible which historically documents the time around the end of the Jewish 70 Year captivity in Babylon and the rebuilding of the Second Jewish Temple in Jerusalem.

The *Apocalypse of Ezra* contains many fascinating prophecies including a sweeping prophecy concerning the past, present, and future role and identity of the ancient Roman Empire, as prophesied by the prophet Daniel in his "Fourth Beast" prophecy.

However, we are going to focus on the future "end time" prophecies which appear to speak of Syria, Russia, Iran, and Arabia, which may now be in the process of being fulfilled.

As a note, I was not even aware of these remarkable prophecies until just recently when I first heard of, and then read, Dr. Ken Johnson's book *Ancient Apocalypse of Ezra: Called 2 Esdras in the KJV 1611* which is a detailed commentary written from a Christian perspective.

For our short study here, we will simply squeeze in a short prophetic summary of the prophecies with a few bullet points and excerpts from Ken Johnson's book. To obtain his fascinating prophetic book studying Ezra's prophecies, go to BibleFacts.org or to Amazon.com and look for Dr. Ken Johnson's book, *Ancient Apocalypse of Ezra: Called 2 Esdras in the KJV 1611*.

**From his book and his site ...**

"The Ezra Apocalypse is the only non-Catholic book included in the KJV 1611 Apocrypha. It contains many prophecies about the end times. Quoted often by the church fathers of the first and second century AD, this apocalypse reveals the rise of Islam. In chapters 11-12 there is a prophecy of a three-headed eagle symbolizing how the Roman Empire would split into three empires. The empires would die out and leave three kingdoms ruling in the last days. Chapters 15-16 contain a prophecy of the Dragon Nations of Arabia. This Islamic power devastates Syria to the point that Russia must step in to control the issue. This Syrian war sets the stage for the beginning of the Last Days. The book also contains numerous prophecies about the signs of the birth pangs and details about the Rapture of the church, revealing that the end is near. Brought to you by Bible Facts Ministries, biblefacts.org."

**Dragon Nations of Arabia**

"This prophecy (quoted by church fathers Hippolytus and Ephrem the Syrian) teaches that a terrible religious system (Islam) rises from the Arabian desert. This system is called the "Dragon Nations of Arabia." Toward the beginning of the end times, the Dragon Nations will seek to invade and destroy the land of Syria. They will lose control of their armies, which will morph into a horrible creation destroying all in its path. Right before Syria would be totally devastated a powerful large nation from the North (Russia) enters the war.

"This sounds like the Syrian war that is occurring right now. Whether this is the actual war or a precursor to a great one, one thing we know for sure, Islam is a major player in end time prophecy and the apostasy.

"In the last ten years, we have witnessed the rise of ISIS from the Dragon Nations, along with the devastation of Syria and the beginning of Russia's involvement."

## Iran Joins This Battle in Syria

"Behold a horrible vision
  that appears in the east
  from where the Dragon Nations of Arabia
  will come with many chariots,
  and the multitude of them will be carried
  as the wind upon the Earth.
  All who hear them will fear and tremble (ISIS).
  Also the Iranians ("the Carmanians"),
  raging and wrathful,
  will attack as wild woodland boars,
  and with great power
  will come and join in battle
  with the Dragon Nations.
  They will lay waste to
  a portion of the land of Assyria (Syria)"
(Apocalypse of Ezra 15:28-30)

## Russia and Allies Join This Battle

"Behold clouds from the east and from the North (Russia)
will come unto the south,
and they are very horrible to look upon,
full of wrath and storm."
(Apocalypse of Ezra 15:28-30)

Note: Russia has launched devastating air strikes from Russian airfields which are located east and north of Syria, as well as from Iran to the east of Syria.

***This war in Syria with Russia and Iran may grow ...***
***If so, people on Earth will be afraid and tremble***

"There will be great fearfulness
and trembling upon Earth,
and they who see the wrath
will be afraid, and tremble."
(Apocalypse of Ezra 15:28-30)

### *Where Are We Now?*

What have we *already* seen the following concerning Syria in the news over the past few years ...

- Saudi Arabia and Jordanian backed Islamic (Sunni) forces join to fight against Assad in Syria

- An enigmatic ISIS Islamic (Sunni) army rises ferociously to conquer, slaughter, and destroy all in its path through Assyria (northern Iraq) and Syria

- Islamic factions within Syria start fighting each other, tearing the nation of Syria apart

- Russia and Iran (Shiite Islam) swoop in to save Assad's Syria with a massive influx of men and arms

- The Assyrians (Kurds – Ancient Medes) declare their own state in Syria, Iraq, and Turkey

    (Note: Ezra's prophecy *also* warns Turkey and Iraq (Babylon) will be caught up in this terrible and prophetic war.)

- Russia and Iran start pouring their forces and advanced weaponry in to save Syria.

- Iranian (Hizbullah) forces in Lebanon join the war in Syria (Lebanon is also mentioned in Ezra's prophecy)

*ALL these events appear to be prophesied in the ancient Apocalypse of Ezra.*

**What happens next?**

We don't know for sure.

But, *IF* this *is* the war prophesied by Ezra, it will eventually (and irreversibly) lead the world into the Ezekiel 38-39 invasion of Israel by Russia and Iran, which will in turn trigger *irreversible* events which will lead the world into the Apocalypse and Armageddon.

What we are now seeing may just be a precursor or dress rehearsal for the real thing. We will have to wait and see.

**More about the Apocalypse of Ezra (2 Esdras) from Ken Johnson ...**

"The KJV 1611 Bible was produced by the Anglican Church under the order of King James 1. It contains the Old and New Testaments, totaling sixty-six books. These are the same ones we have in most modern Bibles today. Every major group of Christians (Catholic, Protestant, and Eastern Orthodox) accept these sixty-six books as the inspired Word of God. Between the Old Testament and the New Testament was a section of disputed books. This middle section, called the Apocrypha, contains the books accepted by the Roman Catholics, but disputed by the Anglicans. However, few know that there is one book in the King James Apocrypha that was accepted by the Anglican Church, but disputed by the Roman Catholic Church. You will not find this book in a Roman Catholic Bible today. Rome does not want you to read this book. We will soon discover why. It is the *Apocalypse of Ezra*. (It is because we find many of the prophecies found in this remarkable book deal with what would one day partly become the Roman Catholic Church).

"The *Apocalypse of Ezra* is called *2 Esdras* in the KJV 1611 Bible. The book has a series of visions about theology and the end times written by Ezra …

"We must always judge every extra-biblical text claiming to teach theology or prophecy by the sixty-six books of the Bible. Even if this work is legitimate and contains real prophecy, it still may have been mistranslated either deliberately or by mistake."

(Dr. Ken Johnson *Ancient Apocalypse of Ezra: Called 2 Esdras in the KJV 1611* pp. 6,9 – Kindle version)

# PROPHECIES OF IRAQ (BABYLON)

*"And Babylon (Iraq),
the glory of kingdoms,
the beauty of the Chaldees' excellency,
shall be as when God
overthrew Sodom and Gomorrah.
It shall NEVER be inhabited,
neither shall it be dwelt in
from generation to generation"
(Isaiah 13:19-22)*

## Prophecies

## of

## Iraq

*"Listen, My people
(Jews and Christians),
flee from Babylon.
Save yourselves!
Run from the LORD's
fierce anger."
(Jeremiah 51:45)*

### The Bible is somewhat a tale of two cities: Jerusalem and Babylon

Babylon is described as being the fountain of rebellion against God and God's Word which has spread throughout the whole world. Babylon also represents the global World system today that despises, rejects, and mocks God's Word. God warns of a coming judgment upon Babylon (modern Iraq). From the Bible, it appears Iraq (Babylon) may rise again as a global economic and religious center ... and then will be utterly destroyed and left uninhabitable.

Great prophecies against Iraq (Babylon) are found in the books of Isaiah, Jeremiah, and also in Zechariah (where Babylon is called by its ancient name "Shinar.") In the New Testament we find a fearful prophecy against "Mystery Babylon" in the book of Revelation chapters 17-18 (in the Bible a "mystery" is something that had not yet been revealed in Scripture).

These prophecies concerning Babylon (Iraq) are not easy to interpret or present in a linear or chronological form. Please seek wisdom, a discerning spirit, and search the Scriptures concerning these prophecies.

**It appears the prophecies against Iraq (Babylon) will be fulfilled in 3 Phases ...**

**PHASE 1:**

Iraq (Babylon) would be invaded and conquered by a coalition of many nations led by a nation and leader from "a far country"... from "the end of heaven" (the opposite side of the Earth). This Bible prophecy does not describe the Persian (and Medes) invasion of Babylon when Cyrus the Great conquered Babylon in 539 BC. At that time the Persians diverted the Euphrates river and entered Babylon through the river bed gates on the night of October 12 without damaging the city. Many of the citizens of Babylon did not even know they had been conquered for several days.

This first phase of the Babylon prophecies may represent a yet future invasion of Iraq, or they could be describing the Gulf War I + Gulf War II "coalition" invasions of Iraq (Babylon). Iraq's leader, Saddam Hussein, even described himself as the new Nebuchadnezzar (the ruler of ancient Babylon).

The section of the prophecy where the Medes (modern-day Kurds) from the northern part of Iraq will invade and attack the south in a very brutal war does not appear to have yet been fulfilled. It is hard to tell if this attack by a cruel army from the northern part of Iraq will take place during the "Phase 1" or "Phase 3" portion of the prophecies against Iraq (Babylon), or if the brutalities and massacres in Northern Iraq by the enigmatic ISIS, or the recent move of Iranian-controlled forces (both ISIS and the Iranian forces are very likely under Russian control) into the recently declared oil-rich state of Kurdistan, may have some future bearing upon these prophecies.

**PHASE 2:**
Iraq (Babylon) will then someday rise to become a great economic and religious center of the world ... filled with evil and wickedness. This is reflected by The "Woman" of Revelation 17:1-18 and Zechariah 5:1-11 ... "The Woman who rides the Beast"... "MYSTERY, BABYLON THE GREAT, THE MOTHER OF HARLOTS AND OF THE ABOMINATIONS OF THE EARTH."

This "Woman" will be a coming global all-in-one religious system which will rise along with a global political and monetary system under the leadership of the coming Antichrist. This man will be a very popular and powerful world leader who will soon rise. He will be the Satanic empowered counterfeit Messiah. The Bible warns around the time of the coming Antichrist and just before Armageddon, Iraq (Babylon) will become an economic and religious power in the world. The coming Antichrist (who will first rise in power over 10 nations which were all once part of the ancient Roman Empire) will possibly shift the center of a coming global economic system and the center of a coming global religious system to Iraq (Babylon) under his control and under the control of his powerful religious partner whom the Bible calls "the Second Beast" (Revelation 13:11-12).

**PHASE 3:**
Southern Iraq (Babylon) will be utterly destroyed and left uninhabitable ... forever! The Bible warns Southern Iraq (Babylon), "Shall be as when God overthrew Sodom and Gomorrah" ... "it shall never be inhabited" ... "neither shall it be dwelt in from generation to generation" ... "Babylon will become a heap of rubble" ... "haunted by jackals" ... "it will be an object of horror and contempt" ... "without a single person living there." Iran now exerts control over this area.

## Prophecies from the book of Isaiah

*The Burden Against Babylon (Iraq) ...*

This prophecy was written by the prophet Isaiah around 700 BC, over 2,700 years ago. A complete scroll of the book of Isaiah was found among the Dead Sea Scrolls (over 2,100 years old) and is now in a glass case on full public display in its entirety in Israel for all to see (including these passages).

Also, for those of you who may have any doubts about Babylon (ancient name) and Iraq (modern name) being synonymous, the official international news-site of Iraq which was run by Saddam Hussein's son, Uday Hussein, was named "Babylon News."

Although Babylon (southern Iraq) was conquered by the Medes and the Persians in ancient times, it was conquered in such a way it was never destroyed. In fact, in the past the great city of Babylon was spared and then inhabited by its conquerors, including both Persia and Greece. Saddam Hussein (and now others) have spent hundreds of millions of dollars restoring the ancient city of Babylon, including the palace where the prophet Daniel served and interpreted the "handwriting on the wall" the night before the Persians conquered the city (by sneaking in under the river gates).

*So, the total destruction of Iraq (Babylon) as clearly prophesied in the Bible, is still future!*

This prophecy against Iraq is fascinating and timely. Scoffers and skeptics should take note, for God says He uses prophecy to prove He is who He says He is. The details in this series of prophecies are both remarkable and hard to ignore.

Interestingly, as a note, some of this Bible Prophecy study was first written before the fall of Saddam Hussein, which seems to show these Bible prophecies concerning Iraq are now in process and on schedule.

## What does God say concerning "The burden against Babylon (Iraq)?"

*God first sends a warning ...*

"The burden of Babylon (Iraq),
  which Isaiah the son of Amoz did see
  (meaning this is prophetic)
  Lift ye up a banner
  upon the high mountain,
  exalt the voice unto them,
  shake the hand,
  that they may go into
  the gates of the nobles.
  (Warn them judgment is coming)
  I have commanded My sanctified ones,
  (Sanctified means 'set aside' for God)
  I have also called My mighty ones
  for Mine anger, (a prophetic war)
  even them that rejoice
  in My Highness."
  (God is raising this army)
  (Isaiah 13:1-3)

## God warned He would first gather MANY nations against Iraq

*Gulf War I + Gulf War II?*

"The noise of a multitude in the mountains,
  like as of a great people;
  a tumultuous noise of the
  kingdoms of nations gathered together:
  (39 nations assembled against Iraq in Gulf War I)

the LORD of Armies (hosts)
musters the armies (host) of the battle."
(Isaiah 13:4) (God gathers these armies)

Study your history books and the Bible. Ancient Babylon was conquered by just *two* nations, the Medes and the Persians (led by Cyrus the Persian), *without firing a shot!*

Now, find and study news videos of the Iraq (Gulf) Wars I & II ... the combined "coalition" of 39 separate nations surrounding and invading Iraq was massive!

***Armies from "a far country"..."The end of heaven"***

"They come from a FAR country,
from the end of heaven,
even the LORD,
and the weapons of His indignation,
to destroy the whole land."
(Isaiah 13:5)

Look at a globe to see where the US is compared to Iraq (Babylon), and then study your history books.

***God links Iraq (Babylon) to the coming Apocalypse ...***

"Howl ye;
For the Day of the LORD
is at hand;   (Day of the Lord is another term for the 'Apocalypse')
it shall come as a destruction from the Almighty."
(Isaiah 13:6)

**Fear would grip the Iraqi soldiers and armies.**

*Watch videos of the Iraqi soldiers trying to surrender during Iraq-Gulf War I ...*

"Therefore shall all hands be faint,
and every man's heart shall melt:
And they shall be afraid:
pangs and sorrows shall take hold of them;
they shall be in pain
as a woman that travaileth:
they shall be amazed one at another;
their faces shall be as flames."
(Isaiah 13:7-8)

The Persians took ancient Babylon without a major battle. They first lowered the river by diverting it, and then snuck in at night to capture the Palace. The Babylonian army didn't even know the Palace had fallen and they had been conquered until after it was all over.

### The Bible warns there is still MUCH to come in Iraq (Babylon) ...

The judgment against Iraq (Babylon) is shown as both a precursor and a major part of the coming Apocalypse and Armageddon. The "Day of the Lord" is the term used in the Old Testament (Tanakh) and the New Testament for what many call the Apocalypse or the Great Tribulation. Apparently this coming destruction of Iraq will somehow be linked to the coming Apocalypse and Armageddon when God will judge ALL the nations and people of the world ...

*"Behold,*
*the Day of the LORD cometh, (the Apocalypse)*
*cruel both with wrath and fierce anger,*
*to lay the land desolate:*
and He shall destroy the sinners
thereof out of it.
For the stars of heaven
and the constellations

thereof shall not give their light:
the Sun shall be darkened
in his going forth,
and the Moon shall not
cause her light to shine.
And I (God)
will punish the world for their evil,
and the wicked for their iniquity;
and I will cause the arrogance
of the proud to cease,
(this means all nations and people)
and will lay low
the arrogance (haughtiness) of the terrible.
I will make a man more precious
than fine gold; (very few will survive)
even a man than the golden wedge of Ophir.
*Therefore I (God)*
*will shake the heavens,*
*and the Earth shall remove*
*out of her place,*
*in the wrath of the LORD of Armies (hosts),*
*and in the Day of His Fierce Anger."* (The Apocalypse)
(Isaiah 13:9-13) (Also see Zephaniah chapters 1-2)

God will stir up the Kurds (the ancient Medes) who now live in Northern Iraq (and Iran, and Turkey.) It is interesting that it was the Medes (the Kurds in northern Iraq) who Saddam Hussein used chemical weapons on and killed an estimated 50,000. These same Kurds (Medes) just recently declared themselves an independent nation. Both Turkey and Iran are now enemies of the Kurds.

This army from the north will have no compassion on the men, women, or children, of Southern Iraq, and will not be interested or swayed by money, silver, or gold to stop their deadly march and slaughter ...

"Behold, I will stir up
the Medes (Kurds) against them,
which shall not regard silver;
and as for gold,
they shall not delight in it.
Their bows also shall dash
the young men to pieces;
and they shall have no pity
on the fruit of the womb;
their eye shall not spare children."
(Isaiah 13:17-18)

**Southern Iraq (Babylon) will one day be utterly destroyed ...**

*Afterwards, it will never, ever, be inhabited by man again.*

"And Babylon,
the glory of kingdoms,
the beauty of the Chaldees' excellency,
shall be as when God
overthrew Sodom and Gomorrah.
(Sudden and complete)
*It shall NEVER be inhabited,
neither shall it be dwelt in
from generation to generation*"
(This judgment still lies in the future)
(Isaiah 13:19-22)

**Prophecies from the book of Jeremiah**

*God warned He would one day raise up foreigners from every side to rise against Iraq (Babylon) ...*

"This is what the LORD says:
'I will stir up a destroyer against Babylon
and the people of Babylonia (Iraq).

Foreigners will come and winnow her,
blowing her away as chaff.
They will come from every side
to rise against her in her day of trouble.'"
(Jeremiah 51:1-2) (Study Gulf Wars I & II)

God's judgment against Iraq (Babylon) is not yet complete. Iraq (Babylon) will once again become a powerful enemy against Israel. God explains He will execute this judgment against Iraq (Babylon) because He has *not* forsaken Israel (even though their sin was great) ...

"Don't let the archers
  put on their armor or draw their bows.
No one will be spared!
Young and old alike
will be completely destroyed.
They will fall dead
in the land of the Babylonians,
slashed to death in her streets.
*For the LORD Almighty*
*has not forsaken Israel and Judah.*
*He is still their God,*
*even though their land*
*was filled with sin*
*against the Holy One (Messiah)*
*of Israel."* (Rejection of their Messiah)
(Jeremiah 51:3-5)

**God is calling on ALL who will hear His voice to flee from Iraq.**

As a note: The atrocities which Islamic ISIS committed against the men, women, and children living in Northern Iraq were inhuman and unspeakable. Islamic ISIS *also* recruited its soldiers from many nations around the world ...

*"Flee from Iraq (Babylon)!*
*Save yourselves!*
*Don't get trapped in her punishment!*
It is the LORD's time for vengeance;
He (God) will fully repay her."
(Jeremiah 51:6)

"And I heard another
voice from Heaven saying,
*"Come out of her, My people,*
*lest you share in her sins,*
*and lest you receive*
*of her plagues.*
For her sins
have reached to Heaven,
and God has remembered her iniquities."
(The Bible warns we must *not* love this world)
(Revelation 18:4)

## God will destroy all who desecrated His Temple in Jerusalem

*"This is His vengeance against those*
*who desecrated His Temple.*
(God now calls Christians His *living Temple*)
Raise the battle flag against Babylon!
Reinforce the guard
and station the watchmen.
Prepare an ambush,
*for the LORD will fulfill*
*ALL His plans against Babylon (Iraq)."*
(Jeremiah 51:12-14)

***Southern Iraq (currently controlled by Iranian Shiites) will NEVER again be inhabited after God's judgment is completed against her ...***

"The LORD says to Jerusalem,
  'I will be your lawyer
  to plead your case,
  and I will avenge you.
  I will dry up her river (Euphrates),
  her water supply,
  (see prophecies of the Apocalypse)
  *and Babylon* (in Iraq)
  *will become a heap of rubble,*
  *haunted by jackals.*
  *It will be an object*
  *of horror and contempt,*
  *without a single person living there."*
(Jeremiah 51:36-37)

This portion may project out even further (see "Mystery Babylon" in Revelation 17:1 - 18) to the final judgment and destruction of ALL the nations and people of the world who have turned their backs on God and rejected His offer of escape, shelter, and protection through His Messiah, Jesus Christ ...

"In their drunken feasts,
  (Iraq may not be under Iran's control here)
  the people of Babylon
  roar like lions.
  And while they lie inflamed
  with all their wine,
  I will prepare a different
  kind of feast for them.
  I will make them drink
  until they fall asleep,
  never again to waken," says the LORD.
  (May be during the Antichrist's one-world religion)
"I will bring them
  like lambs to the slaughter,
  like rams and goats

to be sacrificed.
"How Babylon is fallen--great Babylon,
praised throughout the Earth!
The world can scarcely believe
its eyes at her fall!
The sea has risen over Babylon;
she is covered by its waves.
Her cities now lie in ruins;
she is a dry wilderness
where no one lives
or even passes by."
(This has never yet happened )
(Jeremiah 51:38-44)

God AGAIN pleads with all of His lost sheep to return to Him humbly and in faith, through His Son, Jesus Christ. He warns all those living in Iraq (and anywhere in the world) who will hear and believe His Word while there is still time.

*"Listen, My people  (Jews and Christians),*
*flee from Babylon.*
*Save yourselves!*
*Run from the LORD's fierce anger."*
(Jeremiah 51:45)

"Mystery Babylon" in the book of Revelation also included the pleasure, money, and things of this world that people desire more than God and God's Word. It also describes a coming global Religious System which will one day seem like the answer to all the world's problems, but will in fact be led by Satan and the coming Antichrist (and his religious partner) who will slaughter millions and millions of Christians who will come to believe in Jesus Christ after the Rapture, who are promised special blessings in Heaven when they refuse to take the "Mark of the Beast" in order to buy or sell and are killed for their refusal to take the mark.

*Interesting prophetic insight and details are given here ...*

"But do *not* panic when you hear
the *first* rumor of approaching forces.
For rumors will keep coming
year by year.
*Then there will be a time of violence
as the leaders fight against each other.*"
(Carefully watch the events in Iraq)
(Jeremiah 51:46)

*"For the time is surely coming
when I (God) will punish
this great city and all her idols.*
Her whole land will be disgraced,
and her dead will lie in the streets.
The heavens and Earth will rejoice,
for out of the north
will come destroying armies
against Babylon," (southern Iraq)
says the LORD.
*"Just as Babylon
killed the people of Israel
and others throughout the world,
so must her people be killed."*
(Jeremiah 51:47-49)

## Prophecies from the book of Revelation

"After these things
 (after the rise of the Antichrist)
 I saw another angel
 coming down from Heaven,
 having great authority,
 and the Earth was illuminated with his glory.
 And he cried mightily
 with a loud voice, saying,

*"Babylon the great is fallen,*
*is fallen and has become*
*a dwelling place of demons,*
a prison for every foul spirit,
and a cage for every
unclean and hated bird!
For all the nations have drunk
of the wine of the wrath
of her fornication,
the kings of the Earth
have committed fornication with her,
and the merchants of the Earth
have become rich
through the abundance of her luxury."
(Revelation 18:1-3)

*"Therefore her plagues*
*will come in one day --*
*death and mourning and famine.*
*And she will be*
*utterly burned with fire,*
for strong is the Lord God
who judges her.
The kings of the Earth
who committed fornication
and lived luxuriously with her
will weep and lament for her,
when they see
the smoke of her burning,
standing at a distance
for fear of her torment, saying,
'Alas, alas, that great city Babylon,
that mighty city!
*For in one hour*
your judgment has come.'
And the merchants of the Earth
will weep and mourn over her,

for no one buys their merchandise anymore:
merchandise of gold and silver,
precious stones and pearls,
fine linen and purple, silk and scarlet."
(Revelation 18:8-12)

## God promises a BLESSING for Assyria (Northern Iraq)

In Isaiah 19:24 there is also a prophecy (in fact a prophetic blessing) concerning "Assyria" (yes, you read it right, Assyria, not Syria.) Nineveh, the ancient capital of Assyria (see the book of Jonah), is located in northern Iraq not far from the modern city of Mosul. Much of Iraq's Christian population is now located in this area (and has been decimated by Islamic ISIS). The people who will be living in the northern Iraq area and who will believe in the Messiah (Jesus Christ) while enduring in faith through the troublesome times and persecutions that lie ahead will be blessed by God and will receive a portion of land that has been set aside with Israel. We are told this blessing will come after Armageddon and the return of Messiah, Jesus Christ.

*"In that Day,* (the 1000-Year reign of Christ)
(*After* the "Apocalypse" when Christ returns)
*Israel will be one of three*
*WITH Egypt and Assyria --*
*a blessing in the midst of the land,*
whom the LORD of Armies (hosts)
shall bless, saying,
"Blessed is Egypt My people,
and Assyria the work of My hands,
and Israel My inheritance."
(Isaiah 19:24-25)  (A blessing is also promised for Egypt)

Bible prophecies tell us that believing Christians in northern Iraq (and in Egypt) who are now suffering will one day be blessed in a mighty and wonderful way!

# The Ancient Roman Empire Will Reunite

*"The ten horns are ten kings
who shall arise from (out of)
this kingdom (the Roman Empire).
And another shall rise after them;
He (the Antichrist)
shall be different from the first ones"
(Daniel 7:24)*

## 10 NATIONS OF THE ROMAN EMPIRE WILL RISE AGAIN

**The Bible warns the final "Empire" on Earth will be a re-united Roman Empire**

In the book of Daniel we find *two* amazing Dreams/Visions which we discover represent a *single prophecy* foretelling the future of all Mankind through the rise of *four* great Empires.

This sweeping prophecy takes us from the days of ancient Babylon all the way to the end of the Age when the "Times of the Gentiles" will be fulfilled and Jesus Christ will then return to rule and fully restore the Earth in peace and beauty.

*"And Jerusalem will be trampled underfoot by the gentiles,*
***UNTIL the times of the gentiles is fulfilled."***
*(Luke 21:24)*

In Daniel 2 we find the 4 great gentile Empires described as a "Great Image" (as Mankind sees them). In Daniel 7 we find them described as voracious "Beasts" (as God sees them).

| Daniel 2 | Empire | Daniel 7 |
|---|---|---|
| Head (Gold) | **Babylon** | Winged Lion |
| Arms/Chest (Silver) | **Persia** | Bear |
| Middle & Thighs (Bronze) | **Greece** | Leopard |
| Legs (Iron) | **Rome I** | Terrible Beast |
| Feet/10 Toes (Iron/Clay) | **Rome II** | 10 Horns |

This prophecy (given twice) warns the *final* prophetic empire will begin with 10 Nations rising out of the Roman Empire. We are *also* told Jesus Christ will then return to destroy it as it gathers all its armies against Jerusalem (Armageddon).

**This coming Roman Empire will include both strong and weak nations ...**

*"Whereas you saw the feet and toes,*
  *partly of clay and partly of iron,*
  *the kingdom (Rome) shall be divided ...*
  *And as the toes and feet*
  *were partly of iron and partly of clay,*
  *So the (re-united) kingdom (Roman Empire)*
  *shall be partly strong and partly fragile."*
(Daniel 2:41-43)

**This will be the "kingdom" of the Antichrist**

*"Then I stood on the sand of the sea.*
  *And I saw a Beast (Satan's Antichrist)*
  *rising up out of the sea,*
  *having seven heads and ten horns,*
  *and on his horns ten crowns,*
  *(Leading a revived Roman Empire of 10 nations)*
  *and on his heads a blasphemous name ...*
  *The dragon (Satan) gave him his power,*
  *his throne, and great authority."*
(Revelation 13:1,2)

**We are *also* told these "seven heads" represent the seven great empires which have ruled over Israel:**

- Egypt
- Assyria
- Babylon
- Persia
- Greece
- Rome
- And finally a Revised Roman Empire

The Bible clearly says *"in the last days"* 10 Nations will rise out of the ancient Roman Empire. They could all rise out of the Western (European) half of the Roman Empire which was based in Rome, as we now see many nations of Europe re-uniting into a powerful European Union. Or, since the Antichrist is also called the "Assyrian," these 10 Nations may rise out of the *Eastern* leg of the Roman Empire which was based out of Constantinople (Turkey) and later fled to Russia.

It is also possible these 10 Nations may be divided between the Western *and* Eastern legs of the ancient Roman Empire.

Others have suggested the 10 nations may rise out of trading blocs of nations, or the United Nations, or even NATO.

**The ten horns represent leaders of these 10 nations, and we are told the "11th" horn will be the coming Antichrist**

*"The ten horns are ten kings*
who shall arise from (out of)
this kingdom (the Roman Empire).
*And another shall rise after them;* (an 11th horn)
he (the Antichrist)
shall be different from the first ones,
and shall subdue three kings ..." (The end begins)
(Daniel 7:24)

It is worth noting that over recent years the leaders of France, Italy, and Germany have ALL called for the need of a "powerful leader" to lead the European Union.

## By Two Witnesses

As we see God giving us this same prophecy twice through two separate dreams/visions in Daniel we can *also* find something similar back in the book of Genesis (chapter 4).

After God revealed to Joseph that the interpretations of the two separate dreams/visions of Pharaoh *both* represent the exact same prophecy, Joseph reveals an interesting fact (or rule) concerning such things when they are repeated twice …

"And the dream was repeated to Pharaoh *twice*
  BECAUSE *the thing is fixed by God,*
  And God will shortly bring it to pass."
  (Genesis 41:32)

Since God has given us this prophecy found in Daniel twice (through two separate dreams) we also know the matter is "fixed" and established by God (meaning it *will* take place!)

So, when the World one day sees 10 Nations of the ancient Roman Empire re-uniting and ruled over by a powerful World leader (the Antichrist), they have been warned the end of the Age (the Apocalypse) is near and Jesus Christ (Messiah) will soon return to defend Jerusalem and utterly destroy the armies of the World who will come against her.

# GLOBAL GOVERNMENT & RELIGION

*"Little children,
it is the last hour;
and as you have heard
that the Antichrist is coming,
even now many antichrists have come,
by which we know that it is the last hour."
(1 John 2:18)*

# GLOBAL ECONOMY & RELIGION
# A COMING WORLD LEADER

*"Little children,
it is the last hour;
and as you have heard
that the Antichrist is coming,
even now many antichrists have come,
by which we know that it is the last hour."*
(1 John 2:18)

### The Coming Antichrist

God warns of a world leader who will soon rise and grow in power. He will lead the world into Armageddon.

This coming world leader has been given around 33 different names and titles in the Bible describing attributes (both in the Old and New Testaments). The best known of the names he has been given is the "Antichrist"...

### He will rise in power rapidly

This coming False Prophet (the Antichrist) will begin by first exerting control over ten nations which were once part of the ancient Roman Empire ...

***He will first control 10 nations of the Roman Empire and he will be "different" from the rest of the nations or leaders in some way ...***

"The ten horns are ten kings
 who shall arise from (out of)
 this kingdom (the Roman Empire)
 *And another shall rise AFTER them;*
 *he (the Antichrist) shall be*

*different from the first ones,*
and shall subdue three kings (nations)"
(The end begins)
(Daniel 7:24)

We don't know what nationality this man will be or what might make him "different." In another prophecy he is described as the "Assyrian" (an area around Syria, Iraq, or Israel's Golan Heights). He may even be considered some kind of alien.

This man will quickly consolidate power over 10 nations which were once part of the Roman Empire, and then will rise in power over the whole world through treaties and war. He will be an absolute liar and deceiver. God warns this man will be empowered by Satan. He will lead the world into the terrors of the Apocalypse.

This coming world leader (a False Prophet) has been given *many* names and titles in the Bible, including one of the best known, yet most misleading - the 'Antichrist.' Although he will be against believing Christians and will oppose God's Word, the world will view him as a great leader and a man of peace.

**He will be Satan's counterfeit messiah ...**

**A "Pseudo-Christ"**

He will use deception and lies to "spin" his web of deceit and to conceal his true motives. Even though he will be indwelt by Satan, the churches at this time will *embrace* him as a "man of god" and a loving "man of peace." The Greek word "Anti-Christ" can accurately be translated "Pseudo-Christ."

This holds true of many churches today, who even now are embracing church leaders who *"no longer endure sound doctrine"* and have *"fallen away"* as "ministers, reverends, and priests." Even though in reality they are "pseudo-shepherds" deceitfully teaching and leading *many* away from God's Word, while they mix Biblical truth in with well-crafted lies (as they powerfully convince many to deny, reject, or ignore parts of God's Word and God's Law, often under the seductive banner of "God is love") ...

"Little children,
*it is the last hour;*
and as you have heard
that the Antichrist is coming,
*even now MANY antichrists have come,*
by which we *know* that it is the last hour."
(1 John 2:18)


"For such are false apostles,
*deceitful* workers,
(Warning: They will look and sound very Christian)
*transforming* themselves
into apostles of Christ.
And no wonder!
*For Satan himself
transforms himself into
an angel of light.*
Therefore it is no great thing
if *his* (Satan's) ministers
*ALSO transform themselves
into ministers of righteousness,* (or reverends or priests)
whose end will be
according to their works."
(2 Corinthians 11:13-15)

*Prophecies tell us this man will not be fully revealed until after the Rapture, when the "Restrainer" is taken out of the way ...*

"For the mystery of lawlessness
  is already at work;
  *only He who now restrains (the Holy Spirit)*
  will do so UNTIL He is taken out of the way.
  (The 'Rapture' and our *escape*)
  And THEN the Lawless One (Antichrist)
  will be revealed,
  whom the Lord will consume
  with the breath of His mouth
  and destroy with the brightness of His coming.
  *The coming of the Lawless One (Antichrist)*
  *is according to the working of Satan,*
  *with all power, signs,*
  *and lying wonders"* (He will perform *miracles!)*
  (2 Thessalonians 2:7-9)

**"He who now restrains"...**

The Bible says that all who believe Jesus Christ died for their sins, was buried, and raised from the dead, and receive Him as their Lord and Savior (who saves us from Hell) are "born again," and are then indwelt by the Holy Spirit. According to the Bible, you cannot separate the Holy Spirit from the believing Christian. This is God's promise.

So, in order to remove "He who now restrains" (the Holy Spirit), God must *also* remove the body of believers who are alive at that time. This is why many believe the man some call the Antichrist cannot be revealed until *after* the Rapture.

## The Beast:
## Satan's Antichrist

The world will soon get the leader it seems to be longing and waiting for. A powerful leader who will be popular, attractive, charismatic, and a great talker whose many words will not be chosen for truth, but for deception. A leader who will kill many Christians ...

"Then I stood on the sand of the sea.
*And I saw a Beast* (Satan's Antichrist)
*rising up out of the sea,* (multitude of peoples)
having seven heads and ten horns, (compare to one of Satan's descriptions below)
*and on his horns ten crowns,*
(These represent 10 nations from the Roman Empire)
and on his heads a blasphemous name ...
*The dragon (Satan) gave him his power,
his throne, and great authority."*
(Revelation 13:1,2)

*He will be indwelt by Satan and will perform miracles ...*

"The coming of the Lawless One (Antichrist)
*is according to the working of Satan,
with all power, signs (miracles),
and lying wonders"*
(2 Thessalonians 2:9-10)

*He will demand to be worshiped ...*

"Then the king (Antichrist)
shall do according to his own will:
*he shall exalt and magnify himself
above every god,*

shall speak blasphemies
against the God of gods,
and shall prosper
*until* the Wrath (the Day of the Lord)
has been accomplished;
for what has been determined
shall be done. (The coming "Apocalypse")
He shall regard neither the God of his fathers
NOR the desire of women,
(he may promote the homosexual agenda)
nor regard any god;
*for he shall exalt himself above them all."*
(Daniel 11:36-37)

"The Son of Perdition, (another title of the Antichrist)
who opposes and exalts himself
above all that is called God or that is worshiped,
*so that he (the Antichrist) sits as God
in the Temple of God,* (a new Jewish Temple *will* be built)
*showing himself that he is God."*
(2 Thessalonians 2:4)


## A One-World Government

*He will rule over the whole world ...*

"It was granted to him
to make war with the saints
and to overcome them
(he will slaughter millions).
*And authority was given him
over every tribe, tongue, and nation."*
(Revelation 13:7)

*A physical description of the Antichrist ...*

> "*Woe to the worthless shepherd,* (the Antichrist)
> who *leaves the flock!* (Jewish? Tribe or area of Dan?)
> *A sword shall be against his arm*
> *and against his right eye;*
> *His* (the Antichrist's) *arm*
> *shall completely wither,*
> *and his right eye*
> *shall be totally blinded.*"
> (Zechariah 11:17)
> (This may happen when he receives his mortal head wound)

As noted, this man whom we call the Antichrist has been given many different titles in the Bible. The term "Antichrist" is somewhat misleading. Misleading in that even though this man will be against Christ, the world will see him as a "pseudo-christ." This future world leader will be Satan's counterfeit Christ. He will be very, very popular in the eyes of the world. The world will view him as a great leader and as a messiah.

**We are told a lot about this future world leader, Satan's counterfeit messiah ...**

- He will be indwelt and empowered by Satan
- He will rise in power over the whole world
- He will conquer through treaties and war
- He will be portrayed as "a man of peace"
- He will be very popular around the world
- He will be a great talker and speech maker
- He will likely be attractive (like King Saul)
- He will not regard the desire of women
- He will receive a seemingly mortal head wound
- His right eye may be blinded
- His arm may be completely withered

- He will appear to be "resurrected"
- He will enforce a 7 year peace plan ('covenant') with Israel
- He will require everyone to receive his 'mark'
- He may help get a new Jewish Temple built
- He will stand in a new Temple to say he is 'God'
  (This event will *trigger* the Great Tribulation)
- He will execute millions of Christians
- He will lead the world into ... Armageddon

## A *Second* Beast ...

### The Antichrist's *RELIGIOUS* partner

"Then I saw *another* beast
coming up out of the Earth,
and he had two horns like a lamb
and spoke like a dragon.
And he exercises all the authority of the
first beast (the Antichrist) in his presence,
and causes the Earth and those who dwell in it
to worship the first beast (Antichrist),
whose deadly (head) wound was healed."
(Revelation 13:11-12)

### A One-World Religion Will Rise

*This coming 'ecumenical' Religious System will one day imprison, torture, and execute millions of believing Christians ...*

The Antichrist will *not* be alone. Another man, *also* empowered by Satan, will rule alongside the Antichrist. This powerful and deadly religious leader or "beast" (as God sees him) will rise to world power with the Antichrist. In this prophecy God reveals some important information and details concerning this religious man of power ...

*"Two horns like a lamb,"* tells us he will emerge with powerful Christian credentials, but *"spoke like a dragon"* tells us he will be controlled and directed by Satan.

This person, along with the religious system he will lead, is also referred to in the book of Revelation as *"The Woman Who Rides the Beast."*

We are warned this all-encompassing, one-world religion will rise to power out of Rome (City of seven hills).

## The *Image* of the Beast

"He was granted power
  to give *breath* (some kind of life-like attributes)
  to the image of the beast,
  that the *image* of the beast (the Antichrist)
  *should both speak and cause
  as many as would NOT worship
  the image of the beast to be KILLED."*
(Revelation 13:15)

This religious leader will create some sort of an "image" of the Antichrist. It may be something very miraculous, or it may be two-thousand year old vocabulary trying to describe some future technology such as robotics, animatronics, or virtual reality.

## A One-World Economy and Monetary System ...

### The *Mark* of the Beast

*"He causes ALL,
both small and great,
rich and poor, free and slave,
to receive a MARK
on their right hand or on their foreheads,
and that NO ONE may buy or sell
except one who has the mark,
or the name of the beast,
or the number of his name."*
(Revelation 13:16-17)

The "mark," the "name," and the "number" may signify some kind of political or economic ranking system.

This prophecy is very crucial for those who have not accepted Jesus Christ as their Lord and will be alive when this law is enacted and enforced. This "mark" will signify a person's *allegiance* to this coming world leader. It may include some kind of tattoo, or implanted microchip with all of your credit card and banking information, we really don't know right now.

### It will not be easy to *refuse* this mark

It will *not* be easy to refuse this mark, whatever it is, for many of you will have families and children that will need to be fed. But, by taking this mark, you will have sealed your eternal fate and doom.

Study this passage. People will receive a mark with his (the Antichrist's) name or his number. This way people are identifying themselves and placing their loyalties with *him*.

One of the early church fathers believed and wrote that the coming Antichrist will be such a liar and deceiver that even *after* taking this mark, most of the average people and families will NOT get the food or things promised, and that they will lose their eternal salvation in Heaven for *nothing*.

There will be no turning back for any who take the "mark, the name of the beast, *or* the number of his name." In God's eyes it is as though you have become *betrothed* to Satan and his Antichrist and it will be *irreversible*.

This mark is a spiritual death sentence for all who take it.

***God will take the sting out of death for these millions who will die in faith while refusing to take "the mark of the Beast," and God wants them to know they will be blessed in Heaven for all eternity …***

"Then I heard a voice from Heaven
 saying to me, "Write:
 *'Blessed are the dead*
 *who die in the Lord*
 *from now on.'"* (this is *during* the Apocalypse)
"Yes," says the Spirit,
"that they may rest from their labors,
 and their works follow them."
 (Revelation 14:13)

"Then I saw the souls
 of those who had been beheaded
 for their witness to Jesus
 and for the Word of God,
 who had *not* worshiped
 the beast (Antichrist) or his image,
 and had *not* received his mark
 on their foreheads or on their hands."
 (Revelation 20:4)

*"I saw under the altar
the souls of those
who had been slain
for the Word of God
and for the testimony
which they held.*
And they cried with a loud voice, saying,
"How long, O Lord, holy and true,
until You judge and avenge our blood
on those who dwell on the Earth?"
Then a white robe
was given to each of them;
and it was said to them that
they should rest a little while longer,
until both the number of their
fellow servants and their brethren,
who would be killed as they were,
was completed."
(Revelation 6:9-11)


## The Bible warns ...

*"Now brother will betray brother to death,*
 and a father his child;
 and children will rise up against parents
 and cause them to be put to death.
*"And you will be hated by all men
for My Name's sake.*
 But he who endures to the end
 shall be saved."  (Into the Kingdom of Heaven)
 (Mark 13:12-13)

**An Enigma ...**

*"Here is wisdom.*
Let him who has understanding
calculate the number
of the Beast (the Antichrist),
for it is the number of a man:
*His number is 666."*
(Revelation 13:18)

*For our safety and protection, Jesus commands all ...*

"*WATCH therefore,*
*and pray ALWAYS*
*that you may be*
*counted worthy*   (Through *HIS* worthiness)
*to ESCAPE*
*all these things*
that *WILL* come to pass."
(Luke 21:36)

**The coming Rapture will suddenly, unexpectedly, and without warning,** *remove* **all believing Christians from the Earth as an** *escape* **from the Antichrist** *and* **from the terrors of the coming Apocalypse.**

**NEXT:**

**What *DOES* the Bible tell us about Satan?**

**The Bible has a *lot* to say about this creature, Satan.**

*Since we are told this coming world leader will be indwelt by the power of Satan, we should learn a little bit more about Satan ...*

God wants us to have knowledge of the enemy. God wants us to know Satan is real and he is powerful. We are told he was the "anointed Cherub who covers." The diligent student of the Bible will discover that Cherubim (plural form of cherub) are at the highest level of rank and order of those created beings called angels. Cherubim are not pudgy little babies with wings as shown in some art. They are powerful! We only know of five that were created. Four now surround the throne of God and the fifth was once the head of this rank until he became filled with violence and pride.

We find in the Bible God goes out of His way to make sure we know Satan was created. We also find in the Bible that God, through the Holy Spirit, goes out of His way to make sure we know Jesus Christ was not created. As we are told in the book of John, "Jesus was the Word that became flesh, and the Word was with God and the Word was God and by Him all things were created." God stepped out of Eternity and placed His Spirit into the form of man, as the Son of Man ... as the Son of God. Satan, with his many names and titles, is the most powerful creature ever created. Jesus defeated Satan at the Cross. The only "person" powerful enough to defeat Satan had to be God Himself, who created Satan. We are told Satan rules the Earth and will rule the Earth until Christ returns to take back that which He purchased with His blood. Don't let anybody convince you Satan and Jesus are some kind of equals, but opposites (such as the Mormons and Jehovah Witnesses now teach).

## *The Bible tells us Satan was created ...*

'Thus says the Lord GOD:
"You (Satan) were the seal of perfection,
*Full of wisdom and perfect in beauty.*
*You were in Eden, the garden of God;*
Every precious stone was your covering:
The sardius, topaz,
and diamond, Beryl, onyx,
and jasper, sapphire, turquoise,
and emerald with gold.
The workmanship of
your timbrels and pipes
*Was prepared FOR you*
*on the day you (Satan) were created*
until wickedness was found in you."
(Ezekiel 28:12-15)

## The Bible clearly tells us *Who* created Satan ...

"*In the beginning was the Word,*
and the Word was with God,
*and the Word WAS God.*
He was with God in the beginning.
*Through Him (Jesus Christ)*
*ALL things were made;*
without Him nothing was made
that has been made."
(John 1:1-3)

"The Son
  is the image of the invisible God,
  the firstborn (head) over all Creation.
  *For in Him (Jesus Christ)*
  *ALL things were created:*
  things in Heaven and on Earth,
  visible and invisible,
  whether thrones or powers
  or rulers or authorities; (These are ranks of angels)
  *ALL things have been Created*
  *through Him and for Him."*
  (Colossians 1:15-16)

There are religions today that say Jesus and Satan were "brothers," or are somehow equal but opposites. The Bible is very clear that Jesus *created* Satan, and that is why we are told that "He who is in us is greater than he who is in the World" (1 John 4:4).

## Satan: "Prince of the Power of the Air"

*Jesus called Satan the "Ruler of this world" and he is also described as "the Prince of the power of the air."*

He is a powerful force. His spirit directs leaders, nations, and people. Satan hates the Jews because they brought forth the Messiah and will be instrumental in His return. Satan hates believing Christians because they love and worship the Messiah. The Bible warns he will try to destroy both. We are told to beware of wolves among the sheep. He often uses those who call themselves Christians or Jews to destroy. This powerful angel is given many names and titles in the Bible ...

- Satan (adversary, enemy) ... (Job 1:6, Jn 13:27)
- Abaddon (Hebrew: Destroyer) ... (Rev 9:11)
- Lucifer (shining one) ... (Isa 14:12)

- Devil (slanderer) ... (Matt 4:1, Luke 4:2, 4:6)
- The ruler of the demons ... (Matt 12:24)
- The god of this age ... (2 Cor 4:4)
- The ruler of this world ... (Jn 12:31, 14:30, 16:11)
- Ruler of the darkness of this age ... (Eph 6:12)
- The anointed cherub who covers ... (Ezek 28:14)
- Apollyon (Greek: Destroyer) ... (Rev 9:11)
- The father of all lies ... (John 8:44)
- The liar ... (John 8:44)
- Lying spirit ... (1 King 22:22)
- The prince of the power of the air ... (Eph 2:2)
- The power of darkness ... (Col 1:13)
- Beelzebub (lord of the flies) ... (Mark 3:22)
- The wicked one ... (Matt 13:19, 13:38)
- The great red dragon ... (Rev 12:3)
- The dragon ... (Rev 12:4,7,13,17,13:2,4, 20:2)
- The great dragon ... (Rev 12:9)
- The murderer ... (John 8:44)
- The accuser ... (Rev 12:10)
- The serpent ... (Gen 3:4, 3:14, 2 Cor 11:3)
- That old serpent ... (Rev 12:9, 20:2)
- The angel of the bottomless pit ... (Rev 9:11)
- The Tempter ... (Matt 4:3, 1 Thes 3:5)

**Satan, the great Red Dragon, filled with unspeakable violence and evil, will one day be cast down to Earth ...**

"And another sign
appeared in Heaven:
behold, a great, fiery red dragon (Satan)
having seven heads and ten horns,
and seven diadems on his heads.
*His tail drew a third
of the stars (angels) of Heaven
and threw them to the Earth."*
(Revelation 12:3-4)

"So the great dragon was cast out,
   that Serpent of old,
   called the Devil and Satan,
   who deceives the whole world;
   *he was cast to the Earth,
   and his angels were cast out with him."*
   (Revelation 12:9)

"For we do *not* wrestle against flesh and blood,
   but against principalities,
   against powers,
   against the rulers
   of the darkness of this age,
   against spiritual hosts of wickedness
   in the heavenly places."
   (these are ranks of angels and demons)
   (Ephesians 6:12)


## The Final Battle

Satan and his angels, the fallen ones, apparently one-third of all angels created, will be cast down to Earth. Before this they roamed both heaven and Earth. Satan and most of his angels are not currently confined in Hell. When Satan is cast down to Earth he will no longer have access to God or Heaven. We are told the Earth is already a spiritual battlefield.

The final battle will be fought on Earth. Many think it will start very soon. We can already feel the heat and stench of Satan's foul breath as we look at the violence, lies, war, and disease spreading across the Earth.

# CHINA AND ALLIES WILL DESTROY 1/3 OF MANKIND

*"Now the number of the army of the horsemen was two hundred million." (Revelation 9:16)*

## CHINA AND ALLIES WILL DESTROY 1/3 OF MANKIND

**"The kings from the East"**

It appears from Bible prophecy that China's power and "sphere of influence" over surrounding nations and armies will continue to grow. We are told China and its allies *will* unleash its deadly weapons of mass destruction . . .

**A "200,000,000 Man Army**

A "200,000,000 man army" will one day rise and unleash their deadly weapons to kill 1/3 of the world's population.

**China will unleash its deadly weapons of mass destruction.**

The following prophecy warns the "army *OF* the horsemen was two hundred million." These "horsemen" may be demonic, or they could be a small division or group within this army of 200,000,000, such as a strategic nuclear weapons division, or they may be brightly painted missiles sitting upon missile launchers. The "two hundred million" is to help identify the nation or area they will rise out of. For the first time in the history of Mankind, one nation, China, can now raise an army of 200,000,000.

For China and its allies to quickly destroy 1/3 of *all* Mankind will require the use of nuclear weapons. The weapons required to fulfill this prophecy could only be produced in the generation alive today. It wasn't until 1999, when Clinton-Gore transferred top-secret U.S. missile technology to China, that China could launch multiple nuclear warheads with pin-point accuracy. It appears the Chinese military is someday going to use these deadly missile and weapons technologies *against us!!*

## One-third of all Mankind on Earth will be killed

*"Now the number
of the army of the horsemen
was two hundred million;*
(For the first time such an army could be raised by China)
I heard the number of them.
And thus I saw the horses in the vision:
those who sat on them
had breastplates of fiery red,
hyacinth blue, and sulfur yellow;
and the heads of the horses
were like the heads of lions;
and out of their mouths came fire,
smoke, and brimstone (like sulfurous volcanic eruptions).
*By these three plagues
**a third** of Mankind was killed*
by the fire and the smoke and the brimstone
which came out of their mouths.
For their power is in their mouth and in their tails;
for their tails are like serpents, having heads;
and with them they do harm."
(These could also be some form of demonic creature)
(Revelation 9:16-19)

The Bible tells us only a small remnant of the population on Earth will survive the coming Apocalypse (the "Great Tribulation"). Although, here, we find *demonic angels* being released, much of the global terror will come from mankind destroying mankind, nation destroying nation, deadly wave after deadly wave. The Holy Spirit goes out of his way to let us know that the day and the hour is real and has already been set.

## China's march to Armageddon

China along with its allies and their vast armies will also one day cross the Euphrates as they march through the oil-rich Middle-East towards Israel *into* the Battle of Armageddon.

"Then the sixth angel sounded:
And I heard a voice
from the four horns of the golden altar which is before God,
saying to the sixth angel who had the trumpet,
*"Release the four angels who are bound
at the great river Euphrates."*
(China is building a new silk road through Iran)
So the four angels, who had been prepared
for the hour and day and month and year,
*were released to kill a third of Mankind."*
(Revelation 9:13-15)

"Then the sixth angel poured out his bowl
on the great river Euphrates,
and its water was dried up,
*so that the way
of the kings from the East
might be prepared.* (A *Chinese* led invasion)
(Note: The vast armies of the Antichrist will then move to either counter or assist this Chinese led invasion)
And I saw three unclean spirits like frogs
coming out of the mouth of the dragon (Satan),
out of the mouth of the beast (the Antichrist),
and out of the mouth of the false prophet.
(The "second" Beast - study 'the coming Antichrist')
*For they are spirits of demons, performing signs,
which go out to the kings of the Earth
and of the whole world,*
to gather them to the battle

of that great Day of God Almighty ...
And they gathered them together
*to the place called in Hebrew,
ARMAGEDDON."*
(Revelation 16:12-16)

## The weapons *will* be used

The weapons will be used. Much of the world will be destroyed. Cities will disappear.

These "kings of the East" will represent only *a small part* of those things which will one day come upon the world.

The coming Battle of Armageddon will be the *last* battle ever fought during this Age of Mankind. The Battle of Armageddon will take place at the very end of that prophetic 7-year period of time sometimes called "The Apocalypse."

## Remember, our future is *already* history!

> *"For I am God,
> and there is no other.
> I am God,
> and there is none like Me,
> Declaring the End from the Beginning,
> and from ancient times
> things that are NOT yet done"*
> *(Isaiah 46:9-10)*

# A Coming Peace Plan For Israel

*"When I heard,
My belly trembled;
My lips quivered at the voice:
Rottenness entered into my bones,
And I trembled in myself,
That I might rest (escape)
In the Day of Trouble."
(Habakkuk 3:16*

# A Coming "Peace Plan" For Israel
## (Tremble!!!)

"Then, he (the coming Antichrist)
*Shall confirm a Peace Plan ("covenant')*
with the many (in Israel)
*For one week* (of years)"
(Daniel 9:26)

A "Peace Plan" will one day be enforced upon Israel.

*This Peace Plan will change the World ... FOREVER!!!*

**The Apocalypse Begins**

The Bible warns of a coming "week of years" (a 7-year period of time) during which most living creatures on Earth will be destroyed. Many call this prophetic 7-year period the "Apocalypse."

This is because the book we now know in English as "The Revelation" of Jesus Christ was first entitled "The Apocalypse" in the original Greek, and the book of Revelation describes in great detail the cataclysmic events which will come upon the Earth during this final "week" of 7-years.

What many people *don't* realize is the Bible warns this coming 7-year period of the Apocalypse will *start* with and will be defined by *a coming Peace Plan* ("Covenant") which will one day be enforced upon nation Israel by a coming World Leader (the Antichrist).

The Bible doesn't say this coming world leader (the Antichrist) writes or formulates this coming Peace Plan, but we are told he will *enforce it* upon Israel.

*The coming 7-Year "Apocalypse" will start on the very day this World Leader will enforce this "covenant" upon Israel!*

You can read more on this coming "Peace Plan" for Israel (and the coming Apocalypse) which is included in a detailed study on the remarkable series of prophecies sometimes called "The 70$^{th}$ Week of Daniel" in the book *"The 7$^{th}$ Day Prophecy"* by the same author.

So, whenever you hear of a new Peace Plan being considered for Israel ... *Tremble!!!* Then, draw near to the Lord in love and in faith, for He will lovingly protect you and your family.

**The Bible also warns to beware of "Peace" Movements ...**

"For you yourselves know perfectly
that the Day of the Lord (the coming "Apocalypse")
so comes as a thief in the night.
**For when they say, "Peace and safety!"**
**then sudden destruction comes upon them,**
*as labor pains upon a pregnant woman.*
*And they shall not escape.*
But you, brethren, (believing Christians)
are *not* in darkness,
so that this Day (the coming 'Apocalypse')
should overtake you as a thief.
(We are warned to *know* prophecy and to "Watch!")
You are all sons of light and sons of the day.
We are not of the night nor of darkness.
*Therefore let us not sleep, as others do,*
**But let us watch and be sober."**
(*Learn* the Bible Prophecies and then *watch* World News!)
(1 Thessalonians 5:2-10)

# God's Promise

*"For God so loved the world
that He gave His only begotten Son,
that whoever believes in Him
should not perish (in Hell)
but have everlasting life (in Heaven)."*

*John 3:16*

## *GOD'S PROMISE . . .*

It has been said that for those who sincerely place their faith and trust in Jesus Christ (Yeshua Ha'Mashiach in Hebrew) to save them from all their sins, this short, trouble filled life on Earth will be the closest thing to Hell we will ever experience. But, for those who reject or ignore Him this short life on Earth will be the closest thing to Heaven ...

Jesus died rejected and alone on the Cross. The Bible tells us that it was not the nails which were driven through His hands and feet that kept Jesus on the Cross, it was His love for you. He willingly and lovingly took the penalty and punishment for *all* of your sins. Each and every one of them, regardless how big or how small. Your debt *paid in full, by Him.* Through God's grace, you simply need to *believe* it and *accept* it. It is free to everybody. It is available to everybody. But, God has given each of us the free will to make our own choice. We must *choose* to accept it. We must choose to believe it. It has to be a conscious decision made by each of us at some point in our life. If, through prayer, we sincerely admit or confess that we have sinned, ask for God's forgiveness, and accept Jesus Christ as our Lord and Savior and His suffering and death on the Cross as *payment* for our sins, regardless of how bad our sins are or how often we have sinned or how long it has been since we have asked for God's forgiveness, and sincerely believe He was raised from the dead the third day, it is not only His Word and Promise that all of our sins will be forgiven and completely forgotten, but God tells us that it is the **only** way we can be forgiven and enter into His Kingdom. He will forgive our failures and has compassion. He will help us to change and be strong when we need to be strong and He will be there and help us through all of life's battles ...
*IF* we ask Him.

The Bible warns *everyone* on Earth is a sinner and *without* a "Savior" will be condemned to Hell - "the *second* death." We are told the execution of this judgment will take place *after* this body dies ...

> "And as it is *appointed*
> for men to die *once,*
> but *after* this the judgment"
> (Hebrews 9:27)

God tells us there is an escape for *every* man, woman, boy, and girl in the world who will simply accept it. It is *this* death (in Hell) that Jesus willingly and lovingly stepped forth from Heaven to save us from.

God has gone to extraordinary lengths and pain to provide a narrow path of escape from the utter darkness, aloneness, and torment of Hell. Jesus completed *all* of the work for us. He was the only one who has ever loved you (and me) enough to *substitute* Himself for you (and me) on the Cross. He suffered and died on the Cross to *save* you from Hell. This is why He is called "Savior."

We cannot enter Heaven because of the good deeds we have done or *think* that we have done. We cannot enter Heaven because we were baptized as a baby or were confirmed into a church. There is no other person here on Earth, regardless of their title or position who can save us, and there is no ritual or donation of money that can provide entrance into Heaven, or provide an escape from the alternative. The gospel (good news) is that *if we simply believe* in our hearts that Jesus suffered and died for *all* of our sins, and that He was buried, then rose again the third day, and ask Him to come into our life as Lord and Savior ... then, our life after death *is certain.*

For if we acknowledge Him as King, we shall enter into His Kingdom. If we deny Him as King, we shall be denied entrance into the Kingdom of Heaven. There *is* life after death. An eternal life beyond anything we can ever imagine ... **it's God's Promise!**

It is simply our *faith* in Jesus Christ. A faith that believes only His Blood on the Cross can wash us clean of all our sins, and only His Resurrection can provide the way to eternal life in the Kingdom of Heaven ...

The "*all* roads (religions) lead to Heaven" or "I've been a good person, so I'll go to Heaven" philosophies are wrong *and* deadly. *Three times* Jesus prayed in the garden just before His Crucifixion, "If it is possible (if there is *ANY other way*), then let this cup (His suffering and death on the Cross) pass from Me." Jesus says, *"I am the way, the truth, and the life (in Heaven), and NO ONE comes to the Father except through Me"* (John 14:6). Jesus Christ stepped forth from Eternity to provide us with a way, the *only* Way into His Kingdom of Heaven. He knew what was about to happen to Him when He prayed in the Garden. If there *was* any other way into Heaven, then Jesus didn't have to suffer and die on the Cross. You see it has *nothing* to do with how good we are (or think we are), for we are all saved through *His* righteousness, not ours. This is the precious gift God offers to us - eternal life in Heaven. We can't buy it, and we can't earn it. "Grace" means getting something we *don't* deserve ... and His gift of life in Heaven is *already* paid for.

The Bible tells us God loves each of us so much that He thinks about us constantly, day and night. His thoughts of us outnumber the grains of sand. A love so deep for us that He even allowed (and watched, heartbroken) His Son, His only begotten Son, sent forth from Heaven, willingly suffer and die *for us* (through an act of love, strength, and courage that is beyond our ability to comprehend), so that *any* who believe in Him will not die, but will enter into His Kingdom, through *His* righteousness, and will share in His glory and inheritance. *But,* He has given to each of us the free will to make our own decision to accept or reject His offer. He loves us and His wish is that *all* would accept His offer. That is why He has made it so simple for us and why it is based on His grace and not our "goodness," lest any of us should boast, or get "puffed up." All we have to do is *accept* it and *believe* it. If we sincerely ask Him into our lives, He will do the rest.

This short period of time which we have on Earth simply gives us the time to choose our own destiny. *Where* we will go after this body dies is *our* choice. The moment our soul or spirit is released we will be both conscious and aware of the decision we made, or didn't make. God freely offers each of us *a gift* of life in Heaven. Our acceptance of His offer, through Christ, comes through faith ...

>"For you are all
>sons of God
>through *faith* in Christ Jesus ...
>There is neither Jew
>nor Greek (non-Jew),
>slave nor free,
>male nor female,
>for you *are all ONE*
>in Christ Jesus"
>(Galatians 3:26,28).

So, no matter who we are or what we are, the *Bible* says our path to Heaven is all the same. We are saved from Hell through our faith and love for Christ Jesus.

Our perception of God and Heaven may now seem a little hazy, but *then* (as soon as this body dies) we will see everything clearly. We're told nobody on Earth will fully understand all these things. As the Apostle Paul tells us we will not see clearly until *after* this body dies ...

> "For now we see as through a glass, darkly,
> but then (*after* we die)
> face to face ..."
> (1 Corinthians 13:12).

If you sincerely ask Jesus into your life He will reveal Himself to you and will warmly welcome you into His Kingdom of Heaven. A Kingdom so beyond our ability to comprehend that Paul tells us there *are no human words* that can describe its peace and beauty ...

> *"No eye has seen,*
> nor ear heard,
> nor have entered into the heart
> (or even the imagination)
> of Man (Mankind ... men and women)
> the things which God
> has prepared (in Heaven)
> *for those who love Him."*
> (1 Corinthians 2:9)

The Apostle Paul was willing to endure terrible pain and suffering as he looked ahead to the life in Heaven God has prepared for all who love Him ...

> "For I consider
> that the sufferings

of this present time (in this life)
are not worthy to be compared
with the glory which shall
be revealed in us (in Heaven)."
(Romans 8:18)

Most of us have a conception that eternity "is just lots of time." This concept is wrong. Eternity in God's Kingdom of Heaven is *disconnected* from our physical property of time (a concept that Einstein and modern physics have helped us understand *a little*). Heaven will be incredibly beautiful, peaceful, exciting, restful, never ending ... and *never* boring! The Bible reveals God's love for each of us, including His gracious offer of citizenship in His Kingdom, as sons and daughters, adopted in grace. All we have to do is accept His offer, through His Son, our Lord and Savior Jesus Christ.

Please remember, God loves you more than words can say. He knows the pain and heartbreak we feel ... for He has felt it, too. The Bible says our spirit inside us will someday "groan" to leave this earthly body. The Bible clearly warns there *will* be difficulties, pain, and suffering in this life, *especially* for those who place their love, faith, trust, and obedience in Jesus Christ. Our real life, in Heaven, is yet future ...

"The Spirit *Himself*
bears witness with our spirit
*that we are children of God,*
and if children, *then heirs* --
heirs of God
and *joint heirs* with Christ,
*IF indeed we suffer with Him*"
(Romans 8:16)

> "Because *NARROW* is the gate,
> and *difficult* is the way
> which leads to life (in Heaven),
> *and there are few who find it."*
> (Matthew 7:14)

## *Jesus is our Hope ...*

Although there are times we may feel alone and abandoned, He will *never* forsake you or leave you. The Bible says the true child of God will find suffering in this life. *Each of us will have our faith tested.* Jesus waits for us to ask Him into our lives to help, to strengthen, to comfort, and to heal. He lovingly wraps His arms around the lonely and the brokenhearted. Jesus will never cast away or turn away any man or woman that willingly comes to Him, regardless of how young or how old, or how good or how bad. Any and all who come to Him with a sincere and humbled heart are welcomed with open arms. "If God is for us, who can be against us?" (Romans 8:31). Jesus *is* God. He now prepares our place in Heaven where there will be no fear, no worries, no pain, no heartbreak, and no tears. He *will* see you through these difficult times. *Trust in Him* ... and with open arms and tears of joy He will be there to welcome us into His Kingdom ... *It's God's Promise!*

# Time to Test

# How To Test

# Bible Prophecy

# Time to Test

## HOW татK TO TEST BIBLE PROPHECY

This book will provide *TWO* powerful ways to test Bible Prophecy. We will show how to test using proven Science and Math principles.

### FIRST: USING SCIENCE

Starting in the 6th Grade, all middle school, high school, and college students from around the world are learning the "Scientific Method" is the *foundation* for all scientific investigation, inquiry, and proof.

The Scientific Method is "neutral" by design. Its sole purpose is to provide a mechanism for skeptics, supporters, and antagonists alike to test *any* idea ("hypothesis") in order to determine whether it is TRUE or FALSE.

For the first time in 2000 years, both skeptics and supporters alike can now *test* the Bible Prophecies by objectively using the Scientific Method.

The Scientific Method is based on *first* picking the idea ("Hypothesis" or personal Theory) you wish to have tested.

**To get started, pick YOUR personal Theory (Hypothesis)**

*1. "The generation alive today is now seeing (and will be seeing) the rise of many Bible Prophecies which will change the world (and our lives) ... FOREVER!"*

*2. "All the prophecies were fulfilled way back in 70 AD when Rome attacked Jerusalem and tore down the Temple."*

*3. "Bible Prophecies are merely allegorical (symbolic) and will have no real effect on our lives."*

4. "Bible Prophecies aren't really relevant today. They are just ancient stories that will never happen as written."

5. "As the Theory of Evolution teaches ... there is nothing to worry about, for tomorrow will be like today, only better!"

Now, let's start what may turn out to be the most amazing adventure of your life ... *and it's all real!!!*

**But, don't forget the basic rule of Science ...**

> *"When the facts disagree with your Theory,*
> *Drop your Theory."*

**Now, Apply the Scientific Method in Four Easy Steps:**

1. *Make a List* of Bible Prophecies
   - Learn what they say and what they warn

2. *Gather Data*
   - Search World News reports
   - Get the facts

3. *Analyze the Data*
   - Determine if the news reports from around the world *support* or *contradict* the hypothesis

4. *Finally, draw your own conclusions from the Data!*


**Scientific Method Bible Prophecy Example:**

Test the *"Russia-Iran Will Invade Israel"* Prophecy:

1. *Learn* what this prophecy says ... *Study* the details
   - Has this coalition of nations *ever* invaded Israel before?

2. *Search* world news headlines (gather your data)
   - Search the news for Russia/Iran/Turkey/Israel
   - Look back for a progression or trend over the years

3. *Study and evaluate the facts* (from your news data)
   - Do news reports support or contradict this prophecy?

4. *Draw your own conclusion!*
   - Are we drawing closer to fulfillment?

**Now, take each one of the 16 Prophecies presented in this book and apply the Scientific Method to each and every one of them in order to test and see how your "theory" from above holds up under objective Scientific scrutiny.**

## NEXT: USING MATHEMATICS

In this section you will learn how to objectively test Bible Prophecy using a sound and proven, yet easy to apply, *mathematical* principle.

We will provide two examples of testing Bible Prophecies by calculating the mathematical probability of just *seven* of the sixteen prophecies we will be examining in this book rising together in *one* generation ... in *today's* generation.

**Choosing the Right Tool**

Starting around the $6^{th}$ or $7^{th}$ grade, students from all around the world are *also* learning to use mathematical probabilities as the basis for accurately forecasting future events.

It appears the 'Compound Probability' method is the optimal mathematical tool to apply for our testing purposes. According to Businessdictionary.com, this technique is used to test "the likeliness of two or more independent events occurring at the same time." Life Insurance companies use Compound Probabilities to estimate life expectancies. Casinos also use this powerful mathematical technique to consistently win millions and even billions of dollars by insuring the odds always stay in their favor.

By using this reliable and efficient statistical tool we will show how to estimate the probability of two or more Bible Prophecies rising at the same time ... in *a single generation*.

**Our objective** is to determine whether or not there is a *statistically significant* mathematical probability that the generation alive today *is* unique and is seeing, and will be seeing, the fulfillment of many remarkable Bible prophecies.

**How It Works ...**
**(It's Much Easier Than You Think)**

1. When flipping a coin there is a 1 in 2 probability of it landing on heads. This would be written as 1/2. Then, to determine the probability of a coin landing on heads *3 times in a row* you would use the Compound Probability method by simply *multiplying* each individual probability as follows:

   1/2 x 1/2 x 1/2 = 1/8 probability  (1 time in 8 tries)

2. The probability of rolling a 5 on a six-sided dice is 1/6. If you wanted to know the probability of rolling the number 5 *three times in a row* on the dice, the probability would be:

   1/6 x 1/6 x 1/6 = 1/216 probability  (1 time in 216 tries)

3. Or, if you wanted to determine the probability of flipping a coin and landing on heads three times in a row *combined* with rolling a dice and getting the number 5 three times in a row, you would again just multiply each single probability:

$$1/2 \times 1/2 \times 1/2 \times 1/6 \times 1/6 \times 1/6 = 1/1728$$

So, the chance of heads landing three times in a row together with the number 5 being rolled three times in a row would be 1 time in 1728 tries, typically written as 1/1728.

4. In weather forecasting, to find the probability of it snowing in both Denver and Boston on the same day when the probability of snow in Denver is 20% and Boston it is 50%:

$$20\% \times 50\% = 10\% \ldots \text{or} \ldots 1/5 \times 1/2 = 1/10$$

## It's Time to Test Real Bible Prophecies Using the Science of Mathematical Probabilities

We will now apply the Compound Probability principle to calculate the probability of just *seven* of these 16 Prophecies rising together in just *one* generation ... in *today's* generation.

## How Long Is a Generation?

We have two Biblical options to choose from ...

Option 1:
 Use a *75-year* average *life span* for each generation

 "The days of our lives are *seventy* years;
 And if by reason of strength they are *eighty* years"
 (Psalm 90:10) (75 is the average of 70 to 80 years)

Option 2:
   Use a *35-year* average *father-child generation*

   "From King David until the captivity in Babylon
   are *fourteen* generations,
   and from the captivity in Babylon until the Messiah
   are *fourteen* generations."
   (Matthew 1:1-17)

Note: David to Messiah was *1000 years*.

   *1000 years ÷ 28 generations = 35 years per generation*

Both of these numbers would be acceptable to test, but for our first example we will use the longer 75 year life span number to conservatively minimize the number of generations.

**How many generations should we use?**

We will divide a well-documented period of time by 75 years to calculate the total number of generations to use as a statistically sound sample for our test.

**Three well-documented *Biblical* time-lines ...**

1. Birth of Jesus Christ ............................ 2000 years ago
2. Israel loses national Sovereignty........... 2500 years ago
3. Abraham called by God ........................ 4000 years ago


**For our first example** we will use the 2500 Year time period noted above as the baseline for each of the seven prophecies. This time-line works well because it is of average length, is well-documented in both secular and Biblical history, and also happens to play a critical role in Bible Prophecy.

**This period started in 587 BC** when Babylon conquered Judah (Israel), destroyed Jerusalem as its capital, and then destroyed the Jewish Temple (which at that time would have been considered one of the 7 Wonders of the Ancient World).

**This marks the time** the children of Israel lost control over the Land, and Israel ceased in its global role as a sovereign nation. Israel was then ruled over by Babylon, Persia, Greece, and Rome who later forcibly Dispersed them around the world. After around 2,500 years, Israel again became a nation in 1948. Then in 1967, also for the first time in 2,500 years, Jerusalem came under Jewish control and once again became the capital of Israel. Both of these events fulfilled amazing prophecies.

**This is extremely important** because not only did it fulfill Bible Prophecies, but almost *all* of the major Bible prophecies *require* Israel to be back in her land with borders *and* with a sovereign government ruled by leaders who *can* negotiate peace treaties, uproot citizens, divide the land, and fight wars.

**Calculate the total number of generations** to use as our sample for the test by simply dividing the 2,500 years by 75 (the average length of our generations):

$$2,500 \div 75 \text{ years} \approx 33 \text{ generations}$$

## Determine The Probability Factor For Each Prophecy

We will now determine the probability of each *individual prophecy* rising during a single generation. We will find how many times the events, alliances, or technologies required to fulfill each prophecy have appeared over the past 33 generations.

*Note on all Israel prophecies:* Israel is easy because we know Israel became a nation with Jerusalem as its capital in 1948/1967. So, the generation alive today is the *only* one in the 33 generations which could fulfill these prophecies.

**1. Israel Back As a Sovereign Nation**

*Probability Factor = 1/33   (1 time in 33 generations)*

**2. Jerusalem Once Again the Capital of Israel**

*Probability Factor = 1/33   (1 time in 33 generations)*

**3. A 'Peace Plan' Will Be Enforced Upon Israel**

*Probability Factor = 1/33   (1 time in 33 generations)*

**4. GAZA "Forsaken" by Israel ... Jews "Uprooted"**

*Probability Factor = 1/33   (1 time in 33 generations)*

**5. Russia-Iran vs. Israel:** This prophecy specifically states that this invasion will take place sometime *after* Israel has been re-gathered into her land as a nation which took place in 1948 (Israel) and 1967 (Jerusalem). Today's generation is the first one in 2,500 years that could see this prophecy fulfilled.

*Probability Factor = 1/33   (1 time in 33 generations)*

**6. Earthquakes In Diverse Places Prophecy:** Most people don't realize the key element to this prophecy is not just that Earthquakes will be intensifying, but the remarkable thing about this prophecy is when Jesus Christ gave this prophecy concerning the hearing of "earthquakes in diverse places" 2000 years ago, it could *only* be fulfilled far in the future when there would be *global* communication technologies such as satellite television, cell phones, and the internet capable of reporting these worldwide events as they happen.

*Probability Factor = 1/33   (1 time in 33 generations)*

**7. China and Allies Prophecy:** For China and its allies to quickly destroy 1/3 of *all* Mankind would require the use of nuclear weapons. The weapons required to fulfill this prophecy could only be produced in the generation alive today. It wasn't until 1999, when Clinton-Gore transferred top-secret U.S. missile technology to China, that China could launch multiple nuclear warheads with pin-point accuracy.

*Probability Factor = 1/33   (1 time in 33 generations)*

**Probability Of Each Individual Prophecy:**

1. Israel back in her land as a sovereign nation ........... 1/33
2. Jerusalem once again the capital of Israel ............... 1/33
3. A 'Peace Plan' to be enforced upon Israel .............. 1/33
4. GAZA "forsaken" by Israel ... Jews "uprooted" .... 1/33
5. Russia and Iran preparing for war against Israel ..... 1/33
6. Earthquakes reported globally in real time ............. 1/33
7. China capable of quickly killing 1/3 of Mankind .... 1/33

**Apply the Compound Probability Test Method**

We will now apply the Compound Probability test method. Simply insert the individual probability values to accurately calculate the probability of these seven prophecies rising together in a single generation ... in *today's* generation:

## A Probability Emerges ...

The Probability of These Events Rising Together in One Generation:

$$1/33 \times 1/33 \times 1/33 \times 1/33 \times 1/33 \times 1/33 \times 1/33 = 1 / 42,618,442,977$$

*A Probability of only 1 Time in 42 Billion Generations!*

This test appears to validate there *is a statistically significant mathematical probability* that the generation alive today *is* unique and *is* seeing, and *will* be seeing, the fulfillment of many remarkable Bible Prophecies that will change the world.

This shouldn't surprise us, for we are told God *will* make it clear to those who know His Word and His prophesies when we are getting close. In 2 Peter 3:9 the Bible also tells us the Lord doesn't want *any* to perish in the coming Apocalypse, and that He has been waiting patiently for many to turn back to Him before it's too late, so they "may be counted worthy to *escape* all these things which will come to pass" (Luke 21:36).

## For The Skeptic in All of Us

But, for the skeptic in all of us, let's significantly *lower* our probability factors to an easier to visualize, but highly improbable and unrealistic range, in order to see what happens.

Think *college* students. Let's say the average age of a college student is 19 years old. It's pretty easy to visualize 19 years. So, let's try reducing our individual prophecy factor down from 1/33 (once in every 33 generations) used in the previous test to only a once in every 19 *years* probability. So, we're going to adjust our test range down from 1 in 33 (1/33) *generations* down to only a *1 in nineteen (1/19) years!*

Let's see if these greatly reduced values can generate a theoretical "bottom-limit" statistical probability which even the most fervent skeptic might find difficult to dispute.

**Reduced Probability Values**

1. Israel back in her land as a sovereign nation ........... *1/19*
2. Jerusalem once again the capital of Israel ............... *1/19*
3. A 'Peace Plan' to be enforced upon Israel .............. *1/19*
4. GAZA "forsaken" by Israel ... Jews "uprooted" .... *1/19*
5. Russia and Iran preparing for war against Israel ..... *1/19*
6. Earthquakes reported globally in real time ............ *1/19*
7. China capable of quickly killing 1/3 of Mankind ... *1/19*

**A New Probability Emerges ...**

$$1/19 \times 1/19 \times 1/19 \times 1/19 \times 1/19 \times 1/19 \times 1/19 =$$

*Only once in every 893,871,739 YEARS!!!*

Now consider the fact that the total span of recorded human history is only *5000 years!* So, even by substituting such an unrealistically lowered value we still find a *highly significant* statistical probability of only 1 in every *893,871,739 years* that a single generation ... *today's* generation ... would live to see just *seven* of these remarkable Bible Prophecies rising!

## *Sixteen* Prophecies

Yet, in the previous chapters you soon discovered *sixteen* significant, timely, and remarkable Bible Prophecies which *all* appear to be quickly rising in a single generation ... in *today's* generation!

## What If These Prophecies Were A Fingerprint?

Some of you Mystery and Detective Story fans might be interested to know that in most courts today a fingerprint with 12-points of matching contact can be used to legally identify and convict a suspect.

You will be able to determine through your own investigation whether or not 12 or more of these Bible Prophecies might act as at least 12-points of contact for a "fingerprint" of this generation.

Could the generation alive today be the one which God has spent so much time and effort describing and preparing us for in the Bible?

We think it is possible, but YOU can prove us wrong!!

## Please Remember ...

The two sample tests above are just examples of tests which you can run yourself. We want *you* in control of setting up your own test parameters. We want those testing these things to feel satisfied with the fairness and equity of the test methods and the results which are objectively attained through them.

# RESOURCES

# RESOURCES

To follow the world news concerning these prophecies, or to learn even more prophecies and to find everything needed to challenge, investigate, and test these Bible Prophecies, you can go to ...

### www.TheProphecies.com
World News + Bible Prophecy

At www.TheProphecies.com, the resources which are freely offered to test these things include many detailed Bible Prophecy Studies, a broad range of significant World News Headlines, links to Global News Sites, and an active Blog.

To find additional prophecy books and Bible studies by Craig Crawford you are welcome to visit:

### www.TheProphecies.com

### and

### www.Amazon.com

Made in the USA
Coppell, TX
04 May 2020